COLOR
IN FASHION

A GUIDE TO COORDINATING FASHION COLORS

Yoko Ogawa / Junko Yamamoto / Ei Kondo

ROCKPORT PUBLISHERS • ROCKPORT, MASSACHUSETTS
Distributed by North Light Books • Cincinnati, Ohio

Printed in Japan

First published in the United
States of America by:
Rockport Publishers, Inc.
P.O. Box 396
5 Smith Street
Rockport, MA 01966
TEL: (508) 546-9590
FAX: (508) 546-7141
ISBN: 0-935603-38-7

First published in Japan as
Fashion Color Coordinate by
Nagaoka Shoten, Inc.
© 1989 by Nagaoka Shoten,
Inc.

English language edition
arranged with Nagaoka
Shoten, Inc. through Japan
Foreign Rights Centre

Authors:
Yoko Ogawa
Junko Yamamoto
Ei Kondo

English language edition
edited and produced by:
Blount & Walker
Visual Communications Inc.
8771 Larwin Lane
Orlando, FL 32817
TEL: (407)677-6303

Distributed in the United
States of America by:
North Light Books
an imprint of
F&W Publications
1507 Dana Avenue
Cincinnati, Ohio 45207
TEL: (800) 289-0963
in Cincinnati: (513) 531-2222
FAX: (513) 531-4744

First Canadian edition 1990
published by Rockport
Publishers, Inc. for:
Firefly Books Ltd.
250 Sparks Avenue
Willowdale, Ontario
M2H 2S4 Canada
TEL: (416) 499-8412
FAX: (416) 499-8313
ISBN: 0-929668-79-8

First Indian edition 1990
published by Rockport
Publishers, Inc. for:
India Book Distributors
107/108 Arcadia
195, Nariman Point
Bombay 400 02J
TEL: 225220
FAX: 022 2872531

First Korean edition 1990
published by Rockport
Publishers, Inc. for:
Chongno Book Center Co.
Ltd.
CPO Box 3973
Seoul, Korea
TEL: 732-2331
FAX: 822-732-9223

First Philippine edition 1990
published by Rockport
Publishers, Inc. for:
National Bookstore
701 Rizal Avenue
Manila, Philippines
TEL: 49-43-06
Telex: 27890 NBS PH

First Singapore edition 1990
published by Rockport
Publishers, Inc. for:
Page One The Designers
Bookshop Pte. Ltd.
6 Raffles Boulevard
#03-128 Marina Square
Singapore 1030
TEL: 339-0288
FAX: 65 339-9828

First Taiwan edition 1990
published by Rockport
Publishers, Inc. for:
Long Sea International
Book Co., Inc.
No. 29 Lane 3 Linyi Street
Taipei, Taiwan R.O.C.
TEL: 394-6497
FAX: 886-2-3968502

First Thailand edition 1990
published by Rockport
Publishers, Inc. for:
Asia Books Co. Ltd.
5 Sukhumvit Soi 61
P.O. Box 11-40
Bangkok, 10110, Thailand
TEL: 391-2880
FAX: 662-381-1821

INTRODUCTION

Perhaps nothing says as much about you as the colors you choose to wear. While a steel-gray suit commands deference and respect, a sage green outfit with cinnabar accents can convey a sense of style and familiarity.

Color gives variety to your expression of style. Just a touch of the right color can add unexpected—and becoming—charms. The right color can add visual excitement to a bland outfit or tie together a lively combination of otherwise conflicting colors.

This book will help you coordinate your wardrobe and find the colors and combinations that both flatter and express your individual taste. It will help you understand the basics of color in fashion and, by giving examples of color combinations that work together, help you create new ensembles from clothes you already own.

Elegant

Refined, sophisticated—and full of
aspirations. These combinations make
you stand out in any crowd.

Emphasize Intelligence

Elegant is a word made for describing just the *right* combination of subtlety and style; combinations that are smart, but still restrained. Red tones form the basis of many of the colors in this family, but black looks good when used as a deep accent to many of the combinations.

Peacock green and royal purple blend well with the visually cool surroundings of the city. Either can be used as the main color; together they are striking, but not overbearing.

A visually warmer, but still elegant solution is to use magenta as a main color with soft lavender accents.

Combining soft colors gives a feeling of affluence. Worn together, rose pink, peach, cream and blue-violet reflect maturity and femininity. They are also more fresh, and less somber, than other colors in this family.

A very refined combination, violet and soft grayish-lilac are reminiscent of classic Japanese color schemes.

Imagination Sweetness

Soft and light color schemes add up to a romantic and innocent look. Their bright tones add a conspicuous sparkle to your image while recalling happy childhood imagery: Laces, frills, amusement parks, toys, sherbert and fluffy marshmallow cream towering over a double-dip ice cream cone.

Orchid pink and fresh spring green create a fresh look that works especially well for thin, willowy types with nicely-tanned skin.

Tinged with nostalgia for a bygone era, lilac, lavender and pale purple can be used with white.

These colors lie close together on the color wheel and coordinating them can be tricky. Notice how pink and cream lighten the visual weight of brick red.

These colors are not close together, but the tonality of the colors is very equal. Adding olive green to pink and yellow ties these two complementary colors together.

Romantic

Simple black and white can suggest the innocence of youth while giving hints of alluring maturity.

Casual

Red is very assertive while black usually suggests restraint. Combined in a sporting outfit, the result is bright, striking and stylish.

Relaxed

Casual doesn't have to mean dressed down. These bright combinations are made by adding hints of natural colors to moderate tones. For a leisurely air, try using the lighter tones as the base color of an ensemble; to dress up casual wear for a night on the town, add accents in colors from the "Sporty" palettes (page 14).

Adding gray to purple makes it warmer and less formal. The combination of purple with orange is both rich and daring, young at heart but with an adult sensibility.

This bold combination of fully-saturated tones strikes the eye as rich, rather than strictly playful. A cold-toned metal accessory will give these colors a mechanical, urban look.

An accent of bottle-green provides a visual bridge between the browns and the yellow in this combination. Spring-like and festive, the colors are also bold and assertive.

Yellow-green as a main color can be balanced with earth tones such as ocher and brown. An accent of Cerulean blue adds a slight twist of urban sophistication.

Natural

Found in the earth, fields and streams, these colors are ideal for outfits that are calm and dignified.

Simple & Warm

These are colors you can see in nature—not the spectacular vermillion of a western sunset, but the dusty gray of a stand of aspens or the crisp cerise of the tender new shoots of a rhododendron. These combinations bring together neutral tints appropriate to earth, sand, water and woods. Don't let these colors get too "muddy," but mix them freely with light gray to give them a more urban and less rural feeling.

A palette of greens reflects the balance of nature. The olive green gives depth and substance to the other two colors and serves as a visual midpoint between them.

The colors of dried earth have a low chroma, or intensity, but together, they can make a sharp impression. Try them for sporting about town in the early fall months.

Peaceful and nostalgic, the warmth of these colors brings to mind a sunny spot in a grassy meadow by mixing soft romantic tones with amber.

This grouping is nice for a sunny winter day and looks good when rendered in high-quality material such as cashmere.

Timeless

There is some value, not to mention comfort, in orthodoxy. No matter what the latest fashion is, these combinations will always be chic and refined, if a bit on the conservative side. Inconspicuous colors with depth exude a quiet elegance.

Traditional

Traditions often serve a good purpose. These combinations have stood the test of time and reflect grace and refinement.

Understated, this combination of warm colors works well for items made of high-quality wool.

A cooler grouping in grayish tones, this palette is appropriate for cool, mild days. Imagine the dark brown as a culotte skirt with the other colors incorporated in a tweed blazer.

To lighten up your look in colder weather, try a spot of yellow, used here to tie together a light tone of brick red and light olive green.

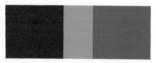

Another cold-weather favorite, this palette could be made up by combining deep purple pants with a dusty-rose sweater and an olive coat.

Vivid & Fresh

Sporty means active and fresh; it means youth, vigor and a certain surety of self-expression. Bright colors, rather than the muted tones of nature or business, are the order of the day and these combinations wear well into the night hours too.

Sporty

Clothes designed for activity and good times can help lift your mood.

Red—favored for sports cars and sports equipment—can be tempered with blue. Adding a hint of purple to the red to make it magenta freshens the look.

Youthful, lively and fresh, these vivid colors are most at home under a brilliant July sun. The orange is brassy and bold—even raffish—while the cream moderates and adds naivete.

There's nothing soft about this combination. Hard-edged and energetic, they give the impression of power.

Cream softens the orange while rich blue tempers the combination. Try blue jeans, a cream pullover and an orange belt, or reverse the scheme with cream pants and blue shirt.

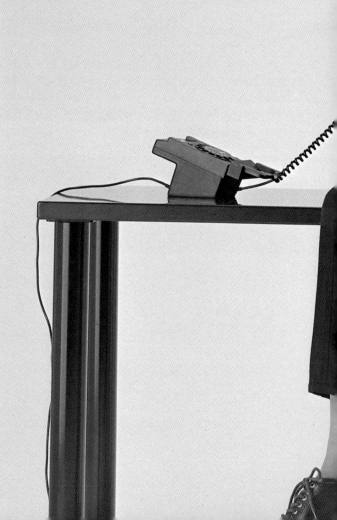

CONTENTS

Basic Color Structure

The human eye is capable of distinguishing millions of individual colors. But all of these, from the deepest, inky black to signal red to bright white, are made up from just seven basic colors: Red, Orange, Yellow, Green, Blue, Indigo and Violet.

If we put these colors in order around a circle, you will see the "color wheel." The wheel can help you visualize how colors complement or contrast, harmonize or clash.

Warm Or Cool? The colors that fall between pure red and pure yellow are called "warm" colors. They excite the senses and make you feel warm. They are the color of fire and the sun. The colors opposite of the warm colors are called "cool" colors. These blue tones are refreshing and calming. They are the color of a clear sky, still water and ice.

Adjacent Colors: The hues which fall next to each other on the wheel and which share a common base are called adjacent. Red and orange both have red in them. Blue and violet both have blue in them. Yellow and yellow-green both have yellow in them.

Split-Complementary: Colors which are opposite one another on the color wheel are called complementary colors. The color adjacent to a color's complementary is its split-complementary. The complement of yellow is violet. Blue and purple are its split complements. Neither violet, purple nor blue has any color in common with yellow.

Triadic: Like red and yellow or red and violet, a relationship that is neither split-complementary nor adjacent is called triadic color. Triadic combinations seem to have a vague common factor. By muting the tones, a very distinguished combination can be made.

Monochromatic Schemes: If we lighten red, we get pink. If we darken it, we get wine. If these tones were used together in an outfit, we would call it monochromatic. Monochromatic combinations are based on one hue, but incorporate more than one shade of that hue.

If the colors of the rainbow are arranged in a circle, the result is a color wheel. This wheel can be used to find each color's complementary colors, adjacent colors and split-complementaries.

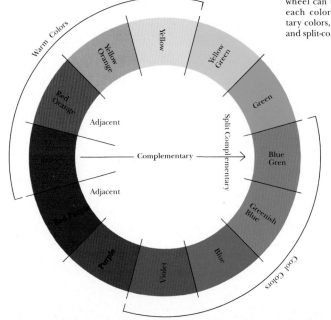

Chroma (Saturation)

Value (Lightness): Chroma is a word used to describe the intensity of a color. The lower the chroma, the lower the brightness. We can say that pale colors which are close to white have a low chroma, and that they are "soft," "light" or "tint" colors.

Colors also have value, which means they are light or dark. An orange color with a low value becomes brown, while given a high value, it becomes peach or salmon.

Tone: We can separate colors into groups with common values and chromas. We say these are "common tones."

The illustrations below show the relationship between value and chroma. Imagine a triangle floating inside of an oval containing the color wheel. Where the triangle's point touches the oval, the color is at full chroma and value. As you look up toward the top of the triangle, the values get lighter. Toward the bottom of the triangle, they get darker. And as you move away from the outside of the oval toward its center, the colors have less chroma, so that they eventually become gray.

Tones can be divided into three broad categories: Tint, shade and dull.

The tones along the top edge of the triangle are "tint" or pastel tones. Those on the bottom edge of the triangle are "shade".

The ones in the center are dull.

There are further divisions of these broad categories into colors which we say are vivid, light, pale, dull, grayish, deep and dark.

Shade colors are made by adding black to a vivid color. Black adds depth. A dark tone close to black will be profound, yet it makes a different impression than pure black.

Dull colors offer a great deal of nuance as they have both moderate chroma and value. They give a natural feeling, as many natural colors are dull.

Tint colors have a low chroma and generally, they look cool to the eye and have a calming effect on color combinations.

This triangle illustrates the relationship between chroma and value. Different tones within the chart fall into categories of color: Tint, shade, vivid, dull, deep, dark or grayish depending on the combination of chroma and value.

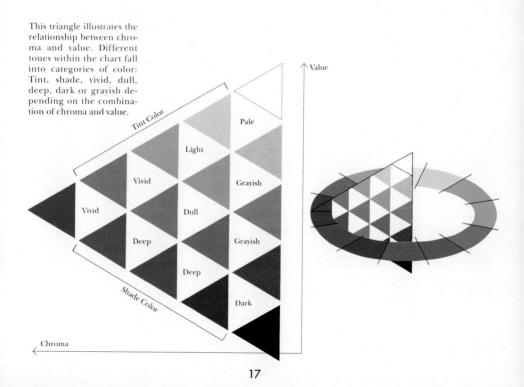

Coordinating Colors By Hue & Tone

Combinations of color illustrate how tones can be varied to change the feeling of an outfit.

Colors such as red, orange and yellow—used at full strength are very vivid. However, if their dull tones are used instead, the effect will be quiet and muted. The light tone (or tint) of orange-red would be peach while a dark tone would be maroon and dull tones would be cinnamon or cocoa.

Ensembles which use different tones of the same color are called monochromatic. An outfit of navy blue, blue and sky blue is one example, one of yellow, yellow ocher and olive is another. Monochromatic schemes bring unity to an outfit; they have a pleasing, natural look. A split-complementary scheme—such as orange and blue—calls attention to the colors and will make you more conspicuous.

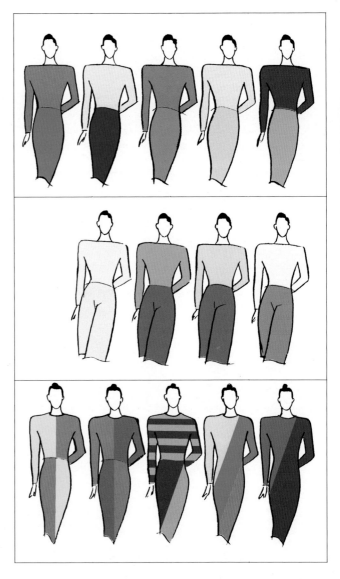

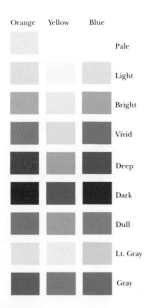

The 27 schemes in the swatches at left are made up from 9 tones of three basic colors. The figure illustrations above show how tones affect the look of a combination. The top row of figures shows tones of two opposing colors, reddish-orange and blue. The middle row shows monochromatic schemes while the bottom shows adjacent colors. The second from right is made of vivid colors while the one at far right is a tonal arrangement.

18

Monochromatic Outfits: Using A Single Color As A Theme

This is an example of an arrangement of quiet colors in reddish-orange. Using lighter tones as the background softens the otherwise brash impression of the orange.

The main color here is blue, with vivid red-orange and yellow added as accents. This brightens the otherwise cool and passive impression created by the blue.

This combination of dark yellow tones is accented with an adjacent color: reddish-orange, which adds spark and vitality.

Split-Complementary Schemes: Conspicuous Choices

Coordinating split-complementary colors usually results in outfits that are conspicuous and colorful. Using a combination of orange and navy blue, for example, results in an outfit that is bright and lively.

But if we change the tones of those colors, as above, the impression is completely different. Here, the navy blue has become sky blue (the light color, or tint, of blue) while the orange has become brown (the dull

tone of orange). This was done to make the warm color darker and cool color lighter, which reverses the normal characteristics of these colors. The result is calm, even though the colors themselves are opposites.

Complementary colors yield the brightest and most conspicuous combinations. Green and red are complementary colors. They are shown here used in tones which have equal levels of brightness. It is easier to coordinate complementaries if they are used in different quantities, rather than in equal, half-and-half proportions.

Yellow and purple are also complementaries. Combining them in unequal proportions makes them blend better as well. Used this way, complementaries can look very chic.

Adjacent Colors Create Mildness

Looking at the color wheel on page 16, colors which are next to or close to each other are called adjacent colors. Because they lie close together on the wheel, they are usually easy to coordinate. At the same time, it is usually best to choose colors which are not so close together that they appear to be the same.

Some colors which are similar but not the same are: red-purple and red; red and orange; orange and yellow; yellow and green; green and blue; blue and purple; and purple and red-purple.

This kind of combination is more interesting than monochromatic schemes, but far less conspicuous

than split-complementary combinations.

The figure at far left (page 22) is dressed in a light tone of red-purple. A red-purple blouse will maintain cohesion in the outfit, while a red blouse will introduce an accent and brighten the overall look.

The middle illustration is an example of using light tones of adjacent colors. The right-hand figure uses adjacent colors of different brightnesses: A very dark, grayed-down yellow is dressed up with bright orange.

The illustrations above show combinations with similar brightnesses.

Triadic Combinations: Making A Mood

It takes a bit more of the adventurous spirit to choose triadic combinations. They are less familiar and don't feel as "safe" as picking straight complementaries or soft adjacent tones.

Triadic colors are those which are 90 degrees apart on the color wheel, for example: green and purple; purple and red; red and yellow; yellow and blue-green; orange and yellow-green; yellow-green and blue; and

blue and red-purple.

Using strong, vivid colors (as at far left) in this arrangement makes for an exotic look. Light and gentle tones of triadic colors can be soft and cool without being cloying or too

sweet (the middle and right illustrations, page 24).

The middle illustration above shows a wine color blouse with an olive-green skirt. The dress at left uses the same colors, but in a dynam- ic pattern. They are neither too loud nor too sober.

It's okay to combine solid-color pieces, but we suggest that they be worn with items that have a pattern, such as checks or stripes. Notice how the polka-dot pattern in the bodice of the dress at right picks up and echoes the color of the belt, shoes and jacket. This enlivens the combination and creates a more sporty look than if the blouse were plain blue-green.

Tonal Coordination: A More Placid Image

All of these colors have a low chroma. The main color will have a grayish, pastel or dark tone. They feel placid because, even though several colors may be used together, all have a significant component of gray.

The example at left shows how dark tones can be used together. The center illustration uses dull tones, while the one at right is composed of light tones.

To make these kinds of combina-tions sparkle, use one bright color with a group of quiet tones or use the tones in unequal amounts.

Complex Coordination: Eccentric Combinations

These combinations may be the most adventurous of all. Eccentric schemes can be created in several ways; each giving a different effect.

The colors are all found in nature, but they are juxtaposed in ways that are unusual. Darkening a light color and lightening a dark color, then wearing them together (as in the center illustration above) will create a cool and mysterious look.

Another example is to combine brown or olive with a light blue, bright blue or violet.

Coordinating The "Mass" Of Colors

In addition to their other characteristics, colors have visual mass and volume.

If you drew two circles of exactly the same size, colored one red and the other cream, the red circle would almost certainly look larger. This impression of volume and weight given by a color is called its mass.

Some colors—such as red—give a very vivid impression even when used in very small amounts. Other colors—such as lilac—have much less mass. They must be used in large amounts to make a vivid impression.

Mass is therefore one of the ways to look at colors when trying to coordinate them. The relationships of mass in a color combination have a remarkable effect on the impression made by the colors.

In coordinating a strong color with a weak one, we can balance them by making the area covered by the strong color smaller and that covered by the weak color larger.

If two colors are very similar—such as red and orange—their mass will be similar as well. Using them in equal proportion will feel balanced, but the effect lacks variation and is uninteresting. When two similar colors are used so that their mass is unbalanced, the combination feels active.

You can get a good feeling for mass by first starting with black, white and gray.

A White and black present the greatest possible degree of contrast. Both colors will come through vividly if they are used in a ration of 7 parts white to 3 parts black. The unequal proportions keeps the black from overpowering the white and makes the combination an active, lively one.

B The two grays used in this combination differ only slightly in value. Slightly more light gray should be used than the dark gray. Grays are very easy to coordinate, but if they look dull to you, add a belt or scarf in a bright accent color.

●When coordinating grays of equal value, use equal amounts of each. Combinations in which the colors have equal chromatic value are often used for clothing.

C Two light grays used together have a mild, harmonized image that a single color can't achieve. However, as above, it helps to add an accent in a brighter color. You can make these colors look richer by using a greater volume of one of them.

D This is a dark, heavy looking combination. The grays have little difference in value, as in example C. Ways to use these combinations include making one color the main color and using the other as an accent or to use different materials for each color.

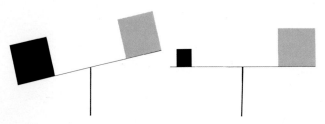

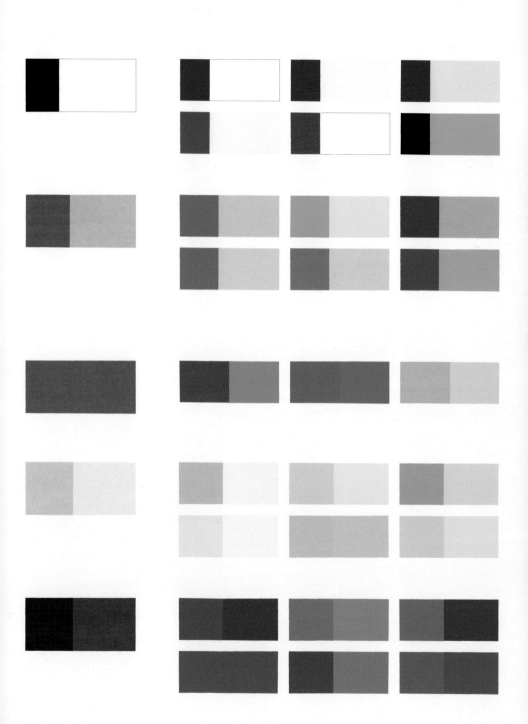

High Contrast

A1 This shows how tonal combination A (page 28) can be used with clothing. When a dark color is used for a skimpy top, the whole outfit looks unbalanced. This may work if the white skirt is made of a striking material.

A2 The fuller silhouette of this skirt helps balance the light color of the bottom with the heavy, strong impression made by the black top.

A3 This is a more natural combination with the heavy color used at the bottom.

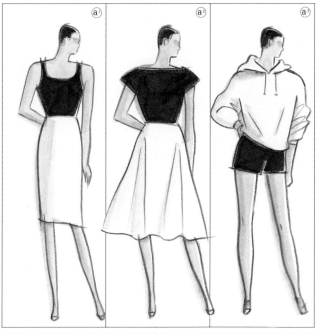

Moderate Contrast

B1 Clothing with moderate contrast can be cut in a variety of shapes, styles and silhouettes. This allows great latitude in choosing accent colors, materials and silhouettes.

B2 This combination is more balanced because, like example A2 above, the volume of the skirt has been increased. Also, a stripe of the darker gray is used at the hem of the skirt to add visual weight at the bottom.

B3 A very natural-feeling arrangement, this group has the light gray on top. A slender silhouette adds to the impression of sharpness. The impression can be changed by wearing the items a little differently: Tucking the sleeves up would look more casual, for example.

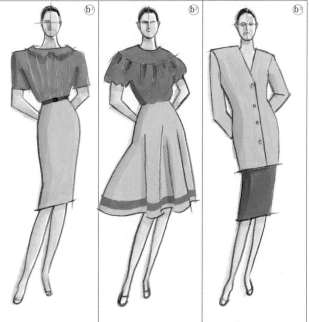

Low Contrast/Light Tones

C1 Using more of the darker of these low-contrast tones helps avoid a look that is too soft.

C2 The ratio of lighter to darker is the same as in C1, but the silhouette is more stylish. Materials such as crepe look good in this combination of colors and styling.

C3 When using low-contrast tones, it's sometimes hard to see where two separate pieces of clothing meet. A belt or scarf will help define the border. If the belt color is a darker tone of the same color family, it will help preserve the feeling of cohesiveness, while a contrasting color will perk up the outfit, making it more lively.

Low Contrast/Dark Tones

D1 When coordinating dark tones, using more of the darker one will emphasize the strength of the darker color.

D2 The ratio of darker to lighter is the same as D1. The choice of materials can make a vast difference in appearance. This outfit, for example, could be made with a plain long-sleeve shirt and a tweed skirt. The contrast of the materials adds vitality to the overall look.

D3 Here, a scarf is used as an accent. Its tones are very different from those used in the outfit, but are from the same color family. Accessories, such as a brooch, can add variety. These will work best if they are very colorful or slightly larger than normal.

Color And Materials

Tweed, serge, canvas, hopsack—all materials reflect light a little differently. Texture and surface gloss change the way a material reflects light and this can make materials look lighter or darker. In coordinating colors for clothing, the types of materials are a primary concern.

The appearance of the color combinations shown in the swatches presented in this book will change according to the material used.

As an example of materials with a high degree of texture contrast, picture satin against tweed. If both were used to make a dark blue dress, the colors would not look at all similar.

Pay special attention to texture when combining colors adjacent to each other on the color wheel. For instance, a gray wool sweater and a khaki gabardine skirt are of different materials, but they both have a flat texture. If the sweater is a cable knit, its texture will contrast nicely with the smoothness of the skirt. If a white shirt and black leather belt are added as accent colors, the textures of the materials make the outfit quiet, but also quite sporty.

Leather and corduroy   Flannel and crepe de chine   Knit and gabardine

Velvet and organdy   Lace and georgette   Tweed and taffeta

Each of these four dresses is the same shade of black, but each has a different nuance, depending on the material. The upper left is black velvet, showing great depth of color; upper right is black lace; lower left is a glossy black satin; lower right is quiet black wool georgette.

Color Swatches

The following pages display a wide variety of color combinations. The names of colors used in this section were taken from *Shokumei Sho Jiten* (*The Small Dictionary of Color Names*) published by the Japan Color Foundation. A color index appears on pages 38-39. The index shows swatches of all the main colors shown on the following pages. If you have a piece of material, match it to these swatches. The page number printed on the swatch will tell you the page on which combinations containing that color appear.

There are 28 groups of colors and four pages of examples for each group.

Most of the groups contain three colors, making it easy to coordinate a wardrobe with main colors, secondary colors and accents.

The theme color is usually shown used for the top piece of an outfit—as a jacket or shirt, for example. The secondary colors are used on bottom, for slacks and skirts.

Choose your theme color first when you begin to coordinate colors, then add colors that enhance it. Don't limit yourself to just one theme color; two-color combinations can be used as a main theme as well.

Experiment. Use these swatches as a starting point, a foundation on which to build your own personal fashion palette.

Colors Used In This Book

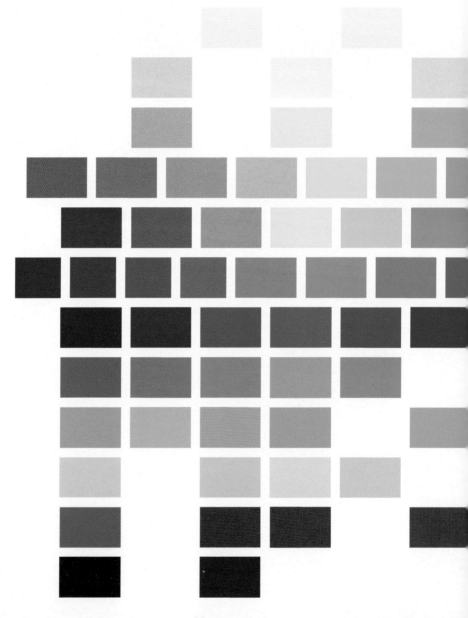

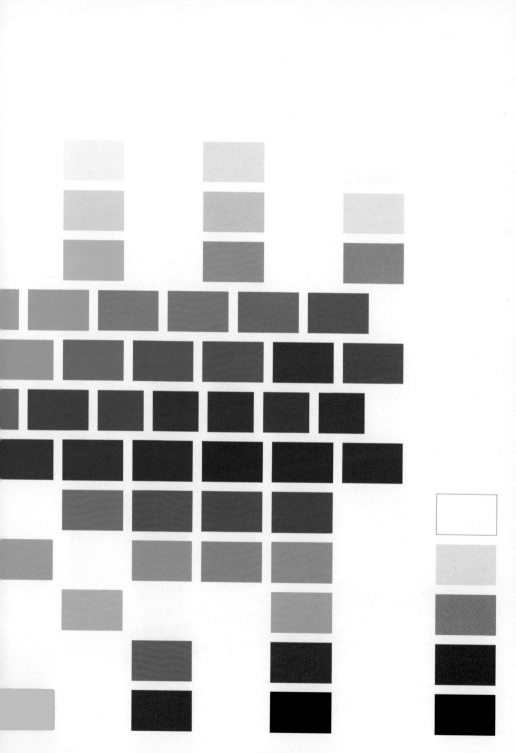

Vivid Red

From left: Red / Rose pink / Vermillion

This group includes a vivid red and two softer ones. In the world about us, we see red in traffic signals, lipstick, apples and ripe tomatoes.

Passion, honesty, vitality and flamboyance are inherent in this bright color; however, a vivid red paired with a soft color is sweet. The nuance of colors in the red family varies with their brightness. As bright red has the same relative color value as medium gray, it is somewhat easier to combine than other bright hues.

Used with yellow as an accessory, red is cheerful. In summer, add white to look fresh. Add a little blue to look extra sporty, and a finely-checked skirt with a red top is very smart.

Vivid colors can be emphasized by pairing them with light tones, soft grayish colors or monochromatic colors. Also, light tones of the split-complementaries harmonize well with red.

Pairing a dull color with red can bring down the outfit, but can work if the dull color is used in a fabric with an obvious texture. Also, if you want to use dull colors with red, try deep green, dark blue or purple. These colors will add depth to the combination

To highlight red, pair it with a grayish color, dark color or monochromatic color. This illustration shows the use of red with brown (which is both dark and dull) and cream. The red jacket adds flair.

1

2

3

4

A vivid red coat and beige one-piece dress make an easy combination when you want to look a little sporty.

Red and green are split complementaries. Although both colors are conspicuous, their tonal values are about equal.

Red and blue are also split complementaries, but the result is more conspicuous when a dark color is used with red.

If you think adjacent colors are hard to coordinate, try using them in a casual outfit. The result may surprise you.

5

6

7

8

This example shows the use of red with beige, rather than the vivid colors shown above.

This combination contains both a triadic and a monochromatic. A tinge of purple is used as a vivid accent.

Black brings an otherwise dull combination of gold and vermillion into style. If the outfit is too dark, add a white accent.

Vermillion—a strong color—can be used with a monochromatic or adjacent color to make a softer, milder impression.

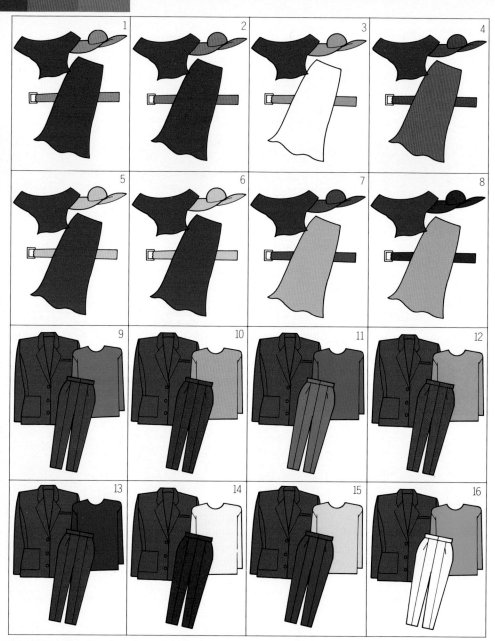

Bright Red: Active And Attractive

The 16 illustrations on this page show arrangements of vivid red. 1-4 have their strength in the similarity of the arrangement. Adding white (3) brings a hint of refreshment in summer. In 5-8, grayish colors have a more casual feeling. In 5 and 6, the red adds power to the beige. The dark grayish colors (9-12) help showcase the brightness of red. Coordinating red with dark tones (13-16) also makes it stand out. The

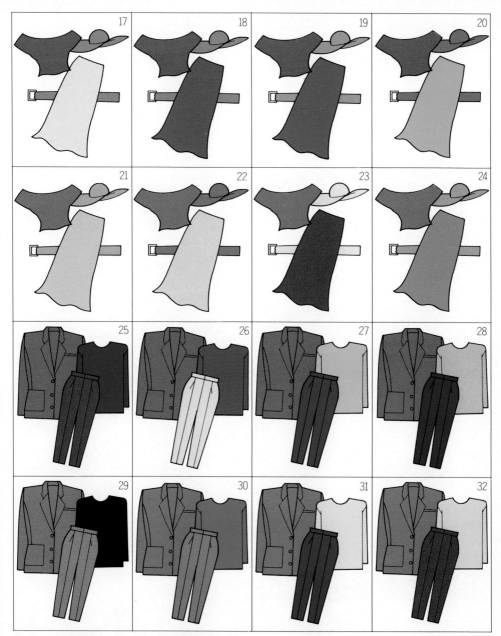

Dress Fashionably In Light Tones Of Red

basic combination of red and dark blue (13) is appropriate anytime. Numbers 17-20 and 25-28 use different tones of red with a variety of light tones. Numbers 21-24 and 29-32 are coordinated with soft, yellowish red. Number 22 doesn't have any one strong, dominating characteristic, but it is fashionable nonetheless. The triadic combination of number 24 has a fresh and challenging look and can be used with beige accents.

These colors range from reddish orange to yellowish-orange and include tangerine, persimmon and pumpkin. All are warm and cheerful.

Reddish-orange is a flamboyant, loud color that gives the image of a flame. Golden orange is the color of the summer sun.

While orange has traditionally been a sporting color, wearing it in the city contrasts nicely with the dull blue and gray tones of concrete and marble. Use an orange hat or scarf to liven up an outfit that is too simple or dull.

Brown and orange seem a natural pair: One is the color of the earth and the other of the sun. The combination works well in the late fall and early winter.

Orange will add a lively feeling when used with red; a lighter feeling if used with yellow or yellow-green.

Reddish-orange is powerful and flamboyant. The color presents a strong image, even when used in small amounts. It will be more conspicuous if used with a dark or dull grayish color.

1

A combination of adjacent colors pairs scarlet with beige. The difference in chroma makes the scarlet stand out.

2

Adding a complementary, such as green, makes a lively and cheerful combination.

3

An adjacent grouping, this outfit mixes scarlet with dark reds. The darker the tones, the more the scarlet will stand out.

4

This outfit mixes scarlet with its other adjacent color, yellow. Again, dark tones are used.

5

Using light tones of adjacent colors can bring a sense of lightness to an otherwise formal outfit.

6

This casual-looking combination is a split-complementary with a large difference in value. It would look good in a pattern.

7

Gray brings calmness to the light tones used for the top and jacket. If the orange looks too loud, try a gray or black jacket.

8

This combination shows a variety of values and chroma. It's light, airy and casual while portraying a fine fashion sense.

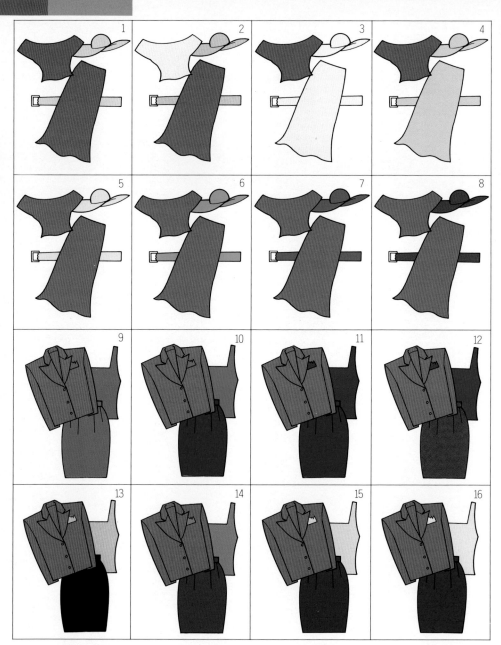

Vivid Orange: Sharp Decision

This orange is lighter than pure red, but it is still vivid and conspicuous. If red shows individuality, then orange expresses energy. Illustrations 1–4 show orange paired with beige and other light tones: the orange looks bright and clear. Examples 5–8 show orange matched with other vivid colors. Wear these at a seaside resort, reflecting the strong colors of the sky and sea. Using orange with deeper tones of the vivid colors (9–12) gives an impression of dynamism. The high-contrast combinations (13–16) are designed for young adults to emphasize individuality. If the outfits look too loud, decrease the amount of orange.

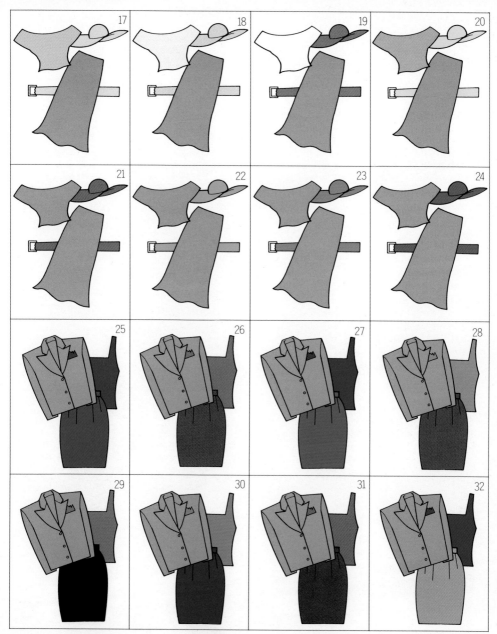

Yellow-Orange Shows Vitality

When using lighter tones of orange with tint colors (17-20), add an accessory of a vivid color to keep the outfit from becoming too light. An accessory—belt, scarf or hat—of a high-chroma color gives substance and solidity to these outfits. The combinations shown in examples 21-24 are casual and would look appropriate at either a seaside or mountain resort. Illustrations 25-28 show how orange harmonizes with dark, grayed or dull colors. The combinations are made using split-complementary and adjacent colors. The bottom row (29-32) illustrates some combinations using orange with a variety of tones from dark to light.

Vivid Yellow

From left: Sunflower / Canary / Lemon yellow

The yellow family includes the brightest colors in the entire spectrum. Daffodils, dandelions and sunflowers are warm, saturated yellows. Canary yellow is soft and gentle. Lemon and grapefruit have a hint of green in them.

Yellow is full of life, and even looks a little innocent. Yellow is fresh and gives an impression of summer. Wear bright yellow in the spring and summer and you'll stand out clearly in the bright natural light. Wear warmer yellow in fall and winter.

Yellow blends beautifully with its opposite color: cool blue. To make a natural combination, wear warm yellow with light, soft tones of sky blue or aqua. Much like white, yellow brightens and adds freshness to any combination.

If used with light or dull tones such as beige or olive, the yellow will be toned down and made mild. But if used with an opposing color, such as blue or purple, the colors will react, creating a dynamic and youthful impression. These combinations will need a secondary color to tie the color scheme together.

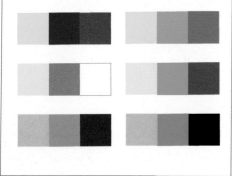

Youthful and active, yellow is the brightest color in the spectrum. It is warm, and reflects the sun and warmth of summer. Tinted with green, yellow looks fresh. When combining yellow, use it with colors which will not overshadow or overpower it.

1. Feminine and spring-like, this combination is clear, warm and light. The monochromatics are used for balance.

2. The values here differ moderately, their chromas being close, but not similar. This combination has a fresh feeling.

3. Useful for a suit or ensemble, these two adjacent colors are both from the warm end of the spectrum.

4. These colors are also adjacent, but the effect is less startling than number 3 and seem to fit together more naturally.

5. Equally adapted to a chic adult outfit or a youthful casual one, the tones must be chosen carefully.

6. This scheme looks fresh because it's not used often. The secondary color is also vivid, so it "stands up" to the yellow.

7. These colors work together because they have green in common. The combination is neither cool nor warm.

8. Using a grayish color as a secondary helps the blue stand out. This combination works well on people of all ages.

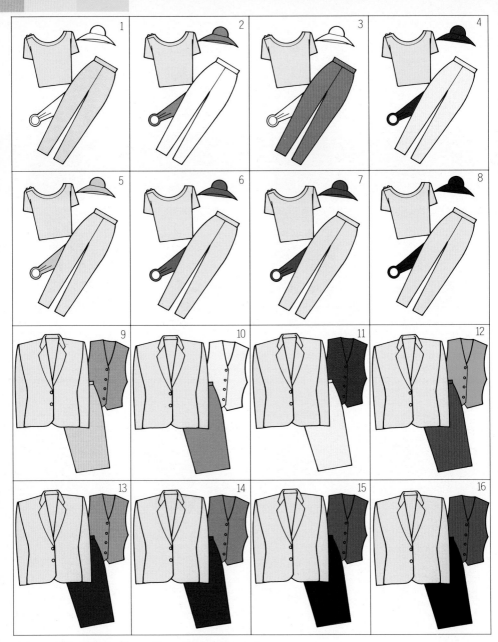

Keep Vivid Yellow Looking Fresh

To use vivid yellow well in your wardrobe, coordinate it with moderate amounts of other colors. Illustrations 1-16 are bright yellow while 17-32 show lemon yellow, which has a hint of green in it. In both cases, the color combinations have been chosen to keep the yellow looking fresh, not muddy. Using it with light colors of white (1-4) gives an impression of liveliness. Bright colors (5-8) are also lively and active. When coordinating yellow with gray or light tint colors (9-12) add a bright secondary color in an accessory or piece of inner clothing to keep the outfit from becoming too quiet, muting the yellow.

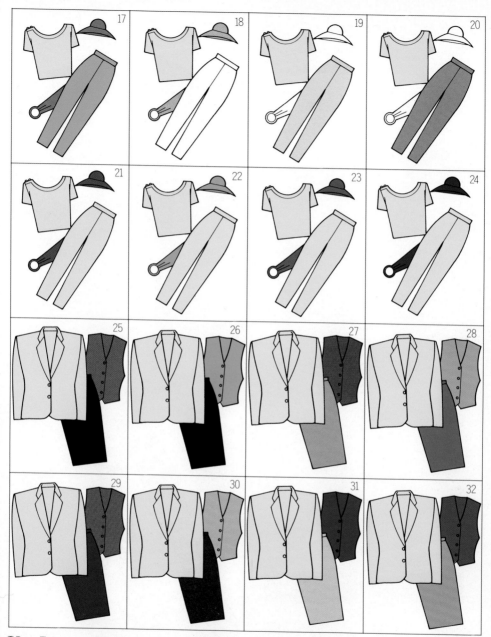

Use Lemon Yellow For A Difference In Tone

Lemon yellow has a hint of green, which opens the door to combining yellow with other colors that share a greenish cast, such as teal and aquamarine and to split complementaries. To tie these together, try using white accessories (19-20). Purple, which is opposite yellow on the color wheel, cools the entire outfit (21). A conspicuous combination (25) makes use of the bright properties of both yellow and red, while 26 shows the effect of green, an adjacent color. The remaining illustrations show combinations of yellow with tint (light) or dull (dark, grayish) colors. These give yellow—normally a casual, sporty color—a demure elegance.

Vivid Green

From left: Fresh Green / Apple green / Emerald

These brilliant greens cover the spectrum we see in the spring, when plants bud and put out their leaves anew. In summer, the new leaves darken to a rich emerald green.

Green looks best when worn with an adjacent color of light, pale or white tone for a cool, vivid impression.

As a main color, yellow-green looks youthful and daring while emerald green is calm and refreshing.

Using green with an opposite, such as red, results in a very bright combination that is balanced because the two have similar brightness and value.

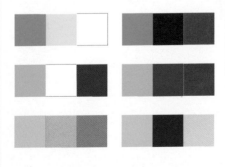

This green is never overly conspicuous, even though it's bright. If you have difficulty coordinating green, try using a monochromatic—black or white—with it.

1

This is a warm combination that looks youthful and vigorous.

2

Combining light green with dark tones gives a casual feeling, while the pink adds a trace of sweetness and femininity.

3

Green and purple are split complementaries. Usually, they make a complex scheme, but here they look simple.

4

Here, two greens are paired with purple. The darkness of the purple helps the light green stand out vividly.

5

Based on light tones, this combination is soft, but still casual and even a bit sporty.

6

Here, beige is used as a bridge to tie together green and purple.

7

Green and blue are adjacent colors and their combination looks clean. The two are often used together for sportswear.

8

Here, red and green both stand out vividly, but they work together because both have similar brightness and value.

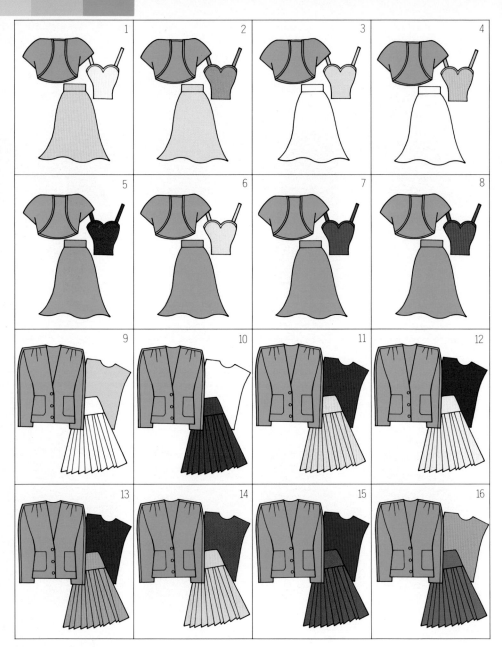

Bright Green: A Refreshing Change

Green is neither cool nor warm. It can be coordinated with a variety of colors. Illustrations 1-16 utilize fresh green, a strong color which, nonetheless, has a calmness to it. Yellow-greens are the softest colors among the bright greens. Illustrations 17-24 show combinations with bright yellow-green, while 25-32 show a green with a touch more blue, making it cooler. Combining bright green with light colors brings out the freshness and keeps the entire outfit looking peaceful. To create more excitement, use a small amount of a vivid secondary color (5-6). The colors in 7 and 8 both share a common tint—blue—with green.

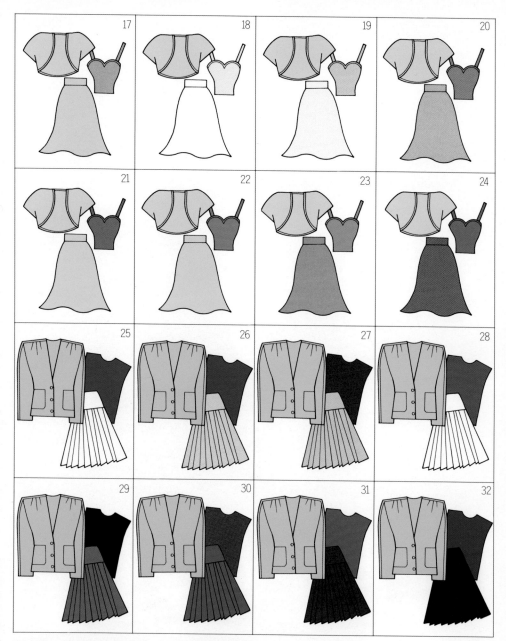

Light Greens—Cool And Invigorating

Yellow-green (9) adds a touch of softness to the combination of bright green and white. The purple tones (11-13) give green an exotic image. While grayed-down tones are usually most appropriate to fall and winter,

by adding green (the combinations shown in 13-16) they can be used throughout the year. Using colors which have a light tint of red in them (17-20) with green softens the otherwise brash look of yellow-green.

Illustrations 21-24 show yellow-green combined with bright colors. Adding darker colors to light green (25-32) gives outfits a calmer—and more mature—aspect. In these cases, a smaller amount of green is used.

This group of bright, blue-tinted greens seems to encompass a wide range of vivid visual images: The deep, profound color of jade, the effervescent coloring of a peacock's plumage, the brilliant aquamarine of a tropical sea.

These bright blue-greens have a mature feeling and are used to best advantage in softer materials, such as tweed.

In winter, wear them with warm colors like coral pink, or for a little stronger impression, tobacco brown.

This family of colors has a long history in Japan, where blue-green is called *aodake-iro* (green bamboo color). It's often used in kimonos paired with yellow-green (*wakadake-iro*: young bamboo color) or paired with gold in costumes for a Kabuki play .

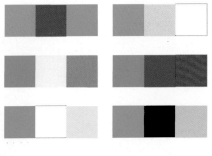

There are many subtle mixtures of blue and green, so choose a shade that works well with the tone of your skin. Adding a warm color will make an outfit based on green more friendly and approachable. Using a variety of textures will help display green to its best advantage.

1

Although this combination is made by intentionally using different colors, its image is softened by using light tints.

2

Giving a somewhat casual appearance, the stronger colors here express a sense of high style without great formality.

3

The cool colors can make this a hard-looking combination. Soft materials, such as tweed, help give it a friendlier look.

4

The use of two brownish tones gives this outfit a bit more masculine feeling.

5

The interplay of the warm, light color with cool green adds interest. Wear this with a white shirt in the spring.

6

This triadic combination is casual, active and sporty. It emphasizes the strength of green, rather than its passivity.

7

When using brown tones with green, pay attention to the cut of the outfit. A simple cut needs accessories to add pizzazz.

8

A feminine-looking combination of split complementaries: Red-purple and green. Choose a delicate style and fabric.

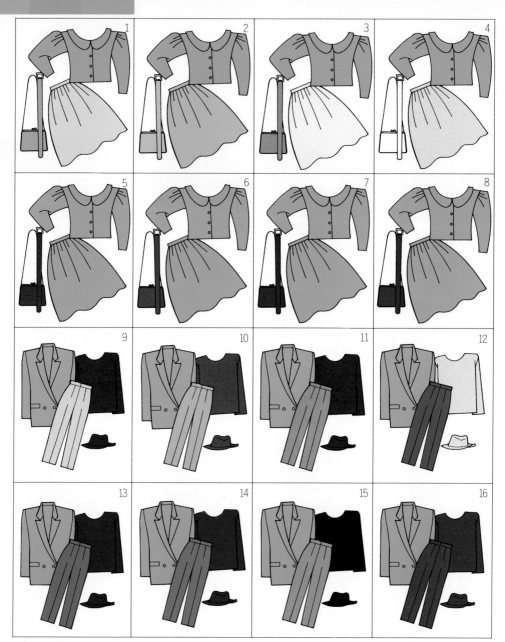

Using Blue-Green With Grayish Tones

Try combining light shades with bluish-green to create a soft impression (1-2). To quiet down an outfit, choose dark-toned accessories (5-8). If you want to use a bright, vivid color to contrast with blue-green, use enough of it to make the contrast clear (9-12). Grayish tones can be the bridge which ties together blue-green and another vivid color. The neutral grays (13-16) can create outfits which have a smart, boyish style to them and display green with a variety of soft tones. Notice how the brown tones in 10 and 16 harmonize with bluish-green. Many shades of brown, from bright to dull can be matched without fear of incompatibility.

58

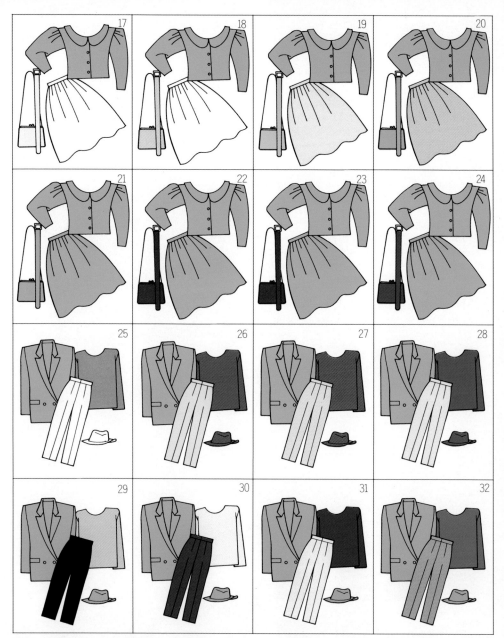

Flexible Combinations For Looking Mature Or Chic

Soft tones used with blue-green can be either dull tones as shown on the preceding page or light tints, as illustrated in 17-20. A dark brown (22) both deepens the outfit and provides a strong point of contrast with the brilliance of blue-green. Bright colors also work with blue-green (25-28) if the shades chosen have a fresh look. Like illustration 8 on page 57, this combination of blue-green, red-purple and light purple gives a soft, femi-nine appearance. When using dark tones with blue-green, those in the brown family seem to harmonize most easily (29-32). The shade of brown can be varied from an antique white tint to deep, tobacco brown.

These blues reflect selections from the full width of the blue spectrum. Cyan is a light blue, and—combined with magenta, yellow and black—is used in full-color printing processes. As such, cyan can be thought of as a "base" color from which other shades of blue are made. Cerulean blue is a lighter, sky-like tone that is bright and clear. Cobalt blue lies towards the purple end of the spectrum.

Blue, especially in darker tones, gives a mental image of wind blowing over the ocean in midsummer. Adding cool ice-green to these colors makes them appear youthful. Combining them with a dark accent, especially brown, creates an image of strength and power.

Using blue with white and red—like the French tricolor—gives a sporty and nautical feeling that is at once friendly and approachable.

Even though a large amount of blue is used, this outfit is not loud or overstated. Blue should be combined in a way that keeps it from looking lonely or monotonous.

1

The light, cool tone of the skirt helps give this outfit an air of innocence.

2

Using a touch of a split complementary—in this case red—helps blue to stand out even when combined with tints.

3

A plain split-complementary combination, this arrangement is appropriate for a summer resort or for city wear.

4

Adding gray tones draws attention to the difference in chroma and highlights the brightness of the blue.

5

Using warm colors with blue decreases its usually cool nature. Try lighter tones to keep the combinations looking bright.

6

Using adjacent and triadic colors with blue can work if they share a common basis; in this case blue itself.

7

In this cheerful combination, both blue and red share the stage. Yellow and red emphasize an active nature.

8

The difference in brightness between these colors highlights blue. This combination also works well for men's wear.

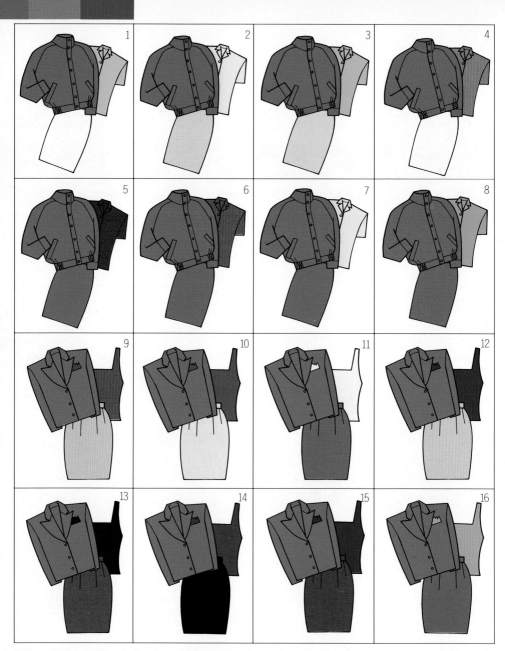

Blue Plus Cool Colors Equals Quietness

By itself, blue has an open feeling. When teamed with warm colors, it really comes alive. Illustrations 1-16 show the freshness of Cerulean blue. Used with light colors (1-4), it looks casual. With warm tones (5-8), it looks youthful and friendly. A more mature look can be achieved by using grayish, rather than vivid, tones (9-16). The light, grayish neutral colors act as a connection between blue and the other colors and also to soft-en the overall brightness of the ensembles. When used with cool tones (13-16), the result is a high-tech kind of feeling. The darker of these tones give more of an impression of masculinity and modernity.

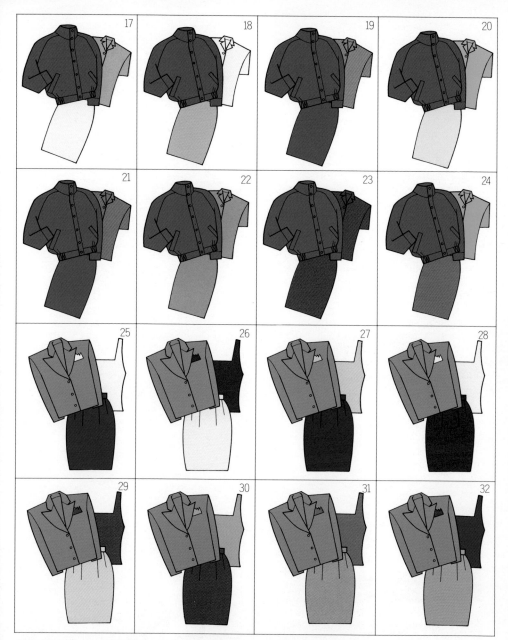

With Warm Colors, Blue Becomes Lively And Active

Although paired with tints of otherwise bright colors, the outfits shown in 17-20 aren't overpowering. The light tones of 17 are youthful and elegant. Active and lively images are provoked by the combinations in 21-24.

The split-complementary scheme in 22 illustrates how the calmness of blue helps it harmonize with its opposing colors. Red-purple (23) is one of blue's triadic colors and together they make an interesting

combination. The soft colors (25-28) give blue a completely different feeling. Here they're paired with cyan, rather than the deeper Cerulean or cobalt blue. Combinations 29-32 are delicate, without an overbearing look.

The tones in this grouping are all named for flowers. The delicacy of these tones is well suited to the soft texture of flower petals, and to soft-textured materials. Purple lies between blue and red on the color wheel. If the shade of purple leans more to the red, it picks up the warmth and passion of this fiery color. If the purple leans more toward blue, it looks cooler, more refined. Violet, which overlaps both of these colors, has both passion and elegance.

Traditionally, the Japanese have preferred cool, bluish purple, while Europeans have leaned toward the red side of the spectrum. Royal purple, for example, has more red than blue.

To wear purple with a casual flair, pair it with a tint of sand beige, khaki or maroon. For a more formal look, add mauve or heliotrope.

Royal purple symbolizes refinement, dignity and sweetness. This color fits well with natural, mild colors. Neutral tints of purple look warm or cool depending on the color they are worn with.

1 Using purple with a natural color—such as beige or hemp—will give a sporty yet elegant effect.

2 With bright pink, the feminine side of purple is emphasized.

3 The deep colors give an impression of strength with the purple serving to brighten the overall look of the outfit.

4 A more daring approach, this combination uses a dull yellow to highlight the purple.

5 Cheerful and lively, this combination uses a variety of light, clear tones.

6 Purple and green are triadic colors which have not traditionally been used together.

7 Using an adjacent color — red—is more naturally harmonious. This combination is sleek and sexy.

8 These colors lie close together on the color wheel, giving an impression of great harmony and coolness.

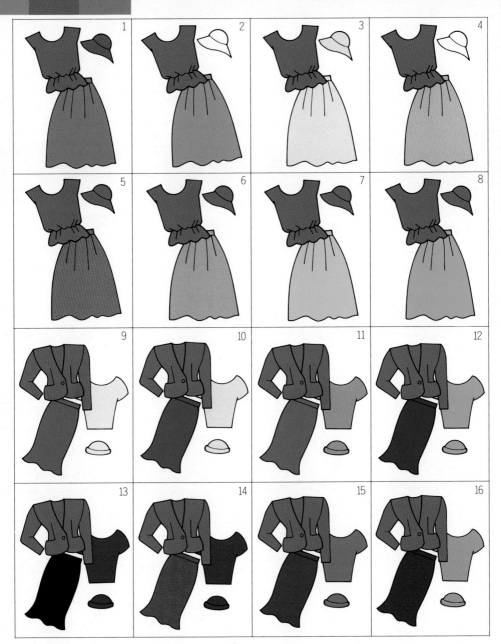

Royal Purple—Passionate And Urbane

Cool, sophisticated and mature all describe the feeling we get from purple. Illustrations 1–16 show the use of violet in schemes that fit naturally with the background of the city. The combinations shown in 17–20 and

25–28 show a cooler side of purple, being tinged with a hint of blue. The illustrations numbered 21–24 and 29–32 use refined light purple. Combination 1 shows purple with red, one of its triadics, as an accent. Numbers 2

and 4 are elegant and would be appropriate to a warm spring day. Numbers 5 and 8 are more casual, fitted to sportswear. To keep these combinations from being too brash, choose quiet accessories.

Shades Of Violet—Shades Of Chic

Soft pink, 9, brings a hint of romance to this multi-piece ensemble. In this case, the purple can be used as a secondary color as well. Combinations 13-16 work well for professional women who want to project a strong image without losing their femininity. The dark tones used in the accessories shown in 21-24 help highlight the purple. Light tones (25-28) make outfits which include purple more casual. These combinations are good for sportswear. Using adjacent colors (29-32) works well with purple. Select the material or style of the accessories carefully to retain the feeling of fashion and elegance which naturally belongs to purple.

Vivid Red-Purple

From left: Iris / Peony / Magenta

Moving from cool to warm—from the cool blue end of the purple spectrum toward red—we encounter this group of rich, striking colors.

In France, the color of azaleas, which belongs in this group, was long considered a very elegant color. In the 1930s a contemporary of Coco Chanel was branded a "revolutionary" after he lightened this popular shade to create "shocking pink."

Historically, purple was thought of as a "royal" color because of the expense of making it from natural materials. Mauve was created accidentally in England as a byproduct of the process that makes quinine, the drug used to treat malaria. It became one of the first very popular synthetic dyes after the press reported that Queen Victoria wore a mauve ensemble while touring an international exposition.

Purple is at home in almost any setting. Paired with black and worn at formal occasions, it is striking. Shiny gold or emerald accessories highlight its qualities.

Purple looks best if monochromatic tones such as black, white or gray accompany it. Purple also works well with brown for casual wear.

1

Light colors set off the purple and create an air of sweetness, accentuated in this case by the soft draping of the outfit.

2

An unfamiliar pair, purple and green are conspicuous when worn together, but no brighter than red and green.

3

The quiet tones of this skirt and scarf are brightened by the addition of a light purple blouse.

4

Brown accessories in a range of styles from casual to formal can be easily combined with purple.

5

A carefree and casual image is created by this green and purple ensemble. Use a light tint of green with white.

6

Navy blue shows off the brilliance of this jacket. This is more fashionable than the usual navy blue and red.

7

A lighter tone of brown makes a sporty combination. This style is simple, but accessories can create an interesting image.

8

White and soft peony purple can be innocent and fresh. Try using these colors with lace to emphasize femininity.

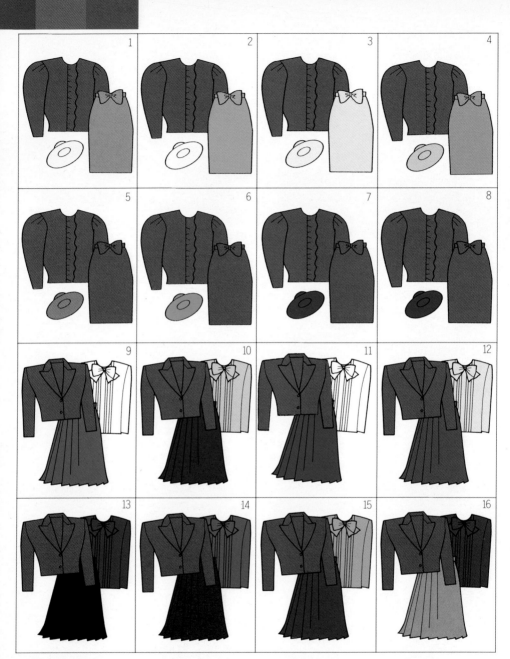

Red-Purple For A Mature And Fashionable Sensibility

These combinations use vivid red-purple, purple and light red-purple. Each has its own peculiar personality. Illustration 1 shows red-purple with its tint, shocking pink, and a monochromatic—white. The tint color softens the effect of the bright red-purple. In 7, the hat is chosen from a deep tone of an adjacent color. The deep bluish tone of the hat in 8 also quiets down the appearance of red-purple, and can be used for other accessories, such as a handbag. The combination shown in 10 is good for formal occasions, while 11 and 15 have a somewhat exotic feeling. Accessories with a slight hint of blue will have a great effect on these.

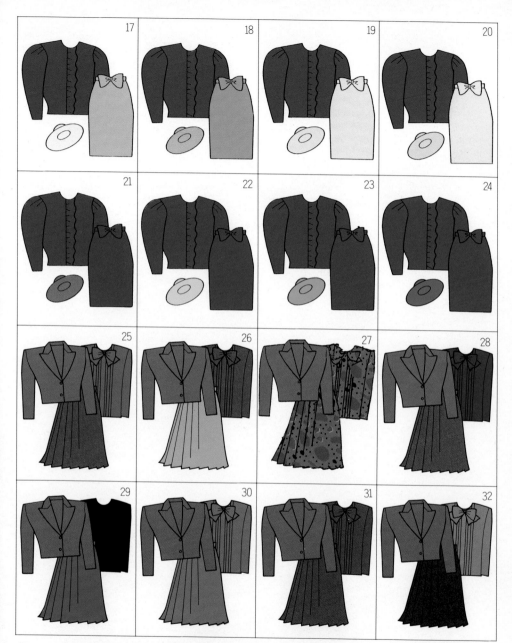

Creative Use Of Light Purple Makes An Outfit Smart

The strong purple used in 17-24 stands out when matched with light tints or neutral colors. When using another strong or contrasting color with purple, neutral accessories help tie the outfit together. The combina-tions in 21-24 are flamboyant and unexpected as these colors have not traditionally been paired with purple. Reserve these for use in the casual atmosphere of a resort or vacation spot and use only a small amount of the accent color. The print in 27 shows how colors react when light purple is used as a background. Brown-gray (30-31) presents a calm and harmonious aspect with light purple.

Pink

From left: Shell pink / Orchid pink / Pale orchid

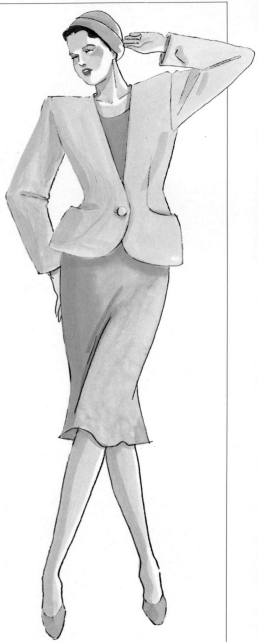

The pinks in this group may remind you of the delicate color of cherry blossoms. They include baby pink, shell pink, coral pink, salmon and peach.

Rose, salmon, peach and coral are the darker tones in this group. Adding a hint of purple results in rose pink and orchid.

The orange-pink tones of peach and salmon match the skin color of many people and make them useful for casual wear. Using them with another shade of pink creates harmony without calling attention to the lightness of pink.

Pink is traditionally thought of as a feminine color. Combine it with soft colors and wear fabrics like cashmere. Here, a tint of an adjacent color is used for heels to highlight and set off the outfit.

1

The combination of light tones gives an impression of innocence.

2

Even though contrasting split-complementary colors are used here, their values are close, rendering them harmonious.

3

The vivid color of this split-complementary scheme is moderated by using a cool tone rather than a warm one.

4

Pink works well with beige, and even with darker tones of brown.

5

Salmon and peach can also be readily combined with light tones, including beige.

6

Though three different colors are used, the ensemble has an overall simplicity and calmness due to the dark tones .

7

Quiet, dark tones of split complementaries highlight the brightness of pink.

8

All three of these colors share a component of red, bringing unity to what might otherwise be a disparate combination.

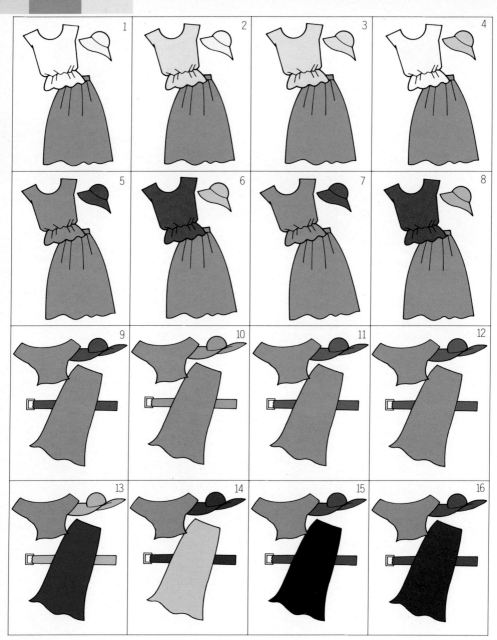

Add Green To Freshen Pink

Use soft accent colors to highlight the sweetness and innocence of pink, or dress it with stronger colors to emphasize its vitality. Flattering feminine styles work best with this color. Illustrations 1-16 show a reddish-pink. Used with a variety of light tones, 1-4 project innocence. The dull colors shown in 5-8 also keep the overall effect soft and feminine. Bright-colored accents, as shown in 9-12, brighten the entire outfit. One way to use pink that makes use of both its softness and its brightness is to use a dull or dark color as a bottom, then add a bright-colored accent piece, one that's not too large or obvious.

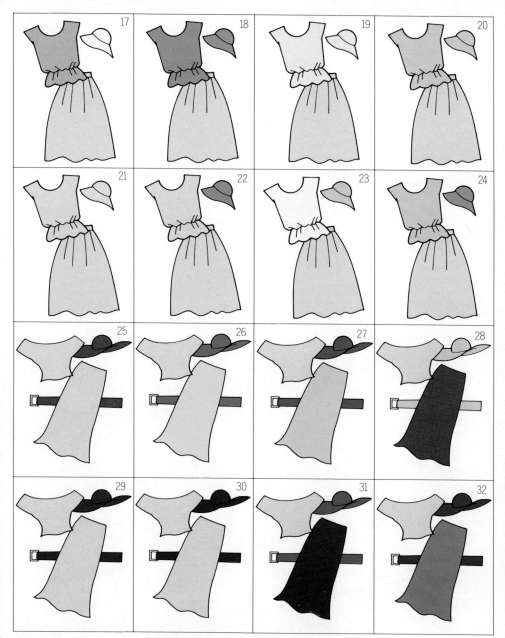

Pink Combines Easily With Many Colors

The illustrations numbered 17-32 show shell pink, which is based on reddish-orange. It may work for you even if you don't look good in rose pink. This pink can be combined in many ways, and will appear romantic, sporty or natural depending on which colors it is used with—i.e. beige, brown, gray, green. The first group (17-20) includes light, clear colors. Pink itself is naturally a clear color, so it also combines well with the grayish tones shown in 21-24. As with rose pink, dark tones can be used to both bolster and calm the usual brightness of pink (29-32).

Light Yellow & Green

From left: Cream / Pale yellow-green / Mint

While this group of light yellows and greens is soft and pleasant, it has less variety of characteristics than other colors. Its impression is usually low-key, natural and relaxed, without the verve of violet or the passion of purple.

The colors range from cream, antique white and ivory to mint, light opal green and light jade green.

Because of the calming effect of these colors, they're often used on interior walls or furnishings. These colors will blend easily with other tones, even though the textures they are used on is dissimilar.

You can assemble outfits by staying within this color group, or, as an alternative, it mixes quite easily with antique rose, cinnamon, camel or khaki.

Cream, which softens the bright yellow in these colors, can be used as a warm white color. By keeping the tonal values of this ensemble close together and light, its image has unity and an overall softness.

1

The colors here are limited, but they are delicate. Mix the textures of the pieces to add interest.

2

This cheerful, warm combination would be a lively choice for wear at a resort or around town.

3

This combination shows a wide divergence in tone and chroma. Dark purple, the opposite of yellow, brings elegance.

4

The colors here are dissimilar also, but the outfit works because the tones are dull, rather than bright.

5

This group shows the possibilities of mint: soft, fresh and cool.

6

Quiet, natural colors work well with mint, showcasing its calmness and brightness.

7

The split-complementaries used in this outfit highlight the mint green nicely.

8

A printed pattern adds interest to the basic mint scheme.

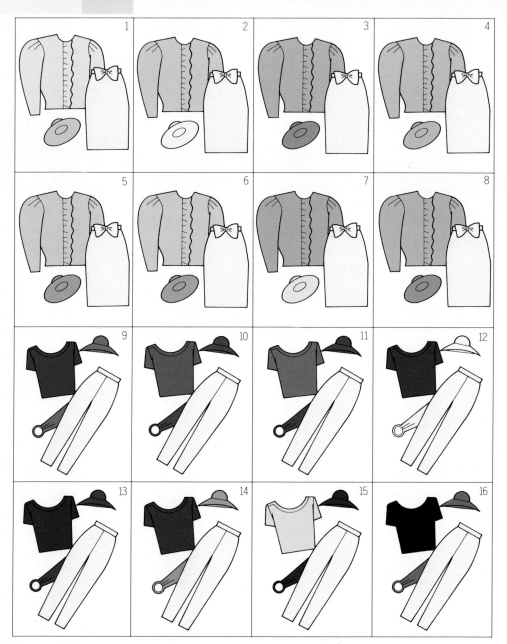

Use Split Complementaries To Highlight Pale Yellow

Colors that are too bright or too vivid easily overshadow yellow, cancelling out its many visual qualities. Illustrations 1-8 are soft and romantic. The secondary colors are close to white in tonal value, so a greater amount of them can be used. The outfits in 9-16 use a cream color based on yellow which is well-suited for use with opposing colors, such as blue or royal purple, or with dark monochromatic tones. Using a small amount of a bright color, in a hat, belt or handbag for instance, can help strengthen the overall impression made by the use of pale yellow with such dark tones. Keep these bright colors to tints, however.

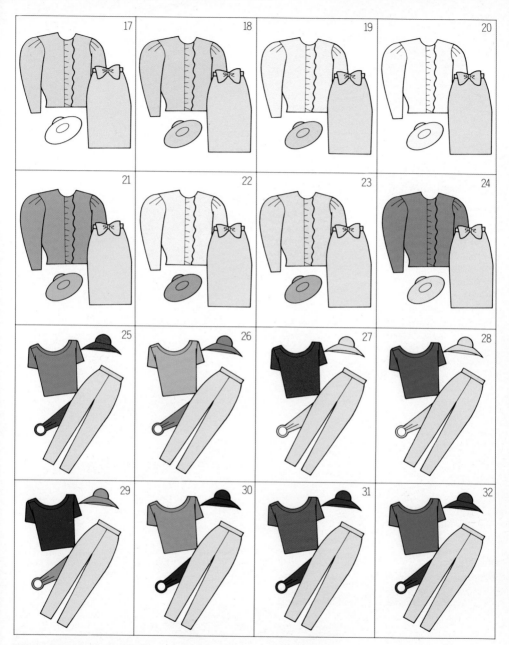

Use Cool Colors To Complement The Freshness Of Green

Mint green is the tint color of green. This is a fresh and pleasant color, but it doesn't have great depth, so that it tends to look odd when combined with some vivid colors. Light or light grayish colors (17-24) work well with mint green. Other soft colors (25-27) also work with mint without overpowering it. The dull or dark tones (26-28) are close to mint green on the color wheel, so they blend well. Also try mint green with vivid green, as shown in 29, or use a monochromatic color. Though light purple and mint green aren't usually suitable together (31) try adding a purple accessory to tie the two together.

Changeable and ephemeral natural phenomena are delicately expressed in these colors, which range from light blue into purple.

Light blue wears well in spring and into early summer. Lavender was very popular in Japan in the early part of this century and is still found in women's kimonos.

During the 19th century, European artists influenced by Japanese lacquerware used this color with coral pink, white, gold or silver.

The color group fits well with browns of many shades. For example, sky blue and beige look natural and gentle. Sky blue and maroon, sepia, khaki or olive are dark, warm colors which make interesting combinations.

These light colors have an overall weakness of impression, so use them on clothing that has more than the usual volume.

The blues in this group remind us of sky and water while the purples recall the blooms of wisteria and lavender. The light colors are passive, and to make them active, try combining them with dark or warm colors.

1 Use sky blue with pink to give a fresh and pure look that wears well in early spring.

2 Though a brighter combination, these colors are all close together on the color wheel.

3 This scheme was made with several tones of blue, relieving what could have been a monotonous arrangement.

4 Using blue with colors that have some cast from the warm end of the spectrum gives it a sporty appeal.

5 When used with monochromatics, the coolness of lavender is emphasized.

6 The differences in these triadic colors helps create an impression of richness.

7 These are all adjacent colors, ranging from deep purple to red purple. The common base makes coordination easier.

8 The vibrant colors used in this triadic combination impart an elegant look.

Light Blue Works Best With Monochromatics Or Adjacents

Light blue can be a weak and passive color, so choose your combinations carefully. The overall impression shouldn't be too cool. Textured materials will help strengthen the image. The quietness of light blue can be disguised by using a larger volume, as in the flared skirt shown in 1–8. Illustrations 1–4 are coordinated using soft colors. When using accent pieces from the same color group, combine them with different tones of blue. A dark skirt (6–7) has a calming effect. Using dull colors for the bottom of the outfit (10–12) gives a stable look, but use a stronger color for accents to preserve the overall impression of vibrancy and energy.

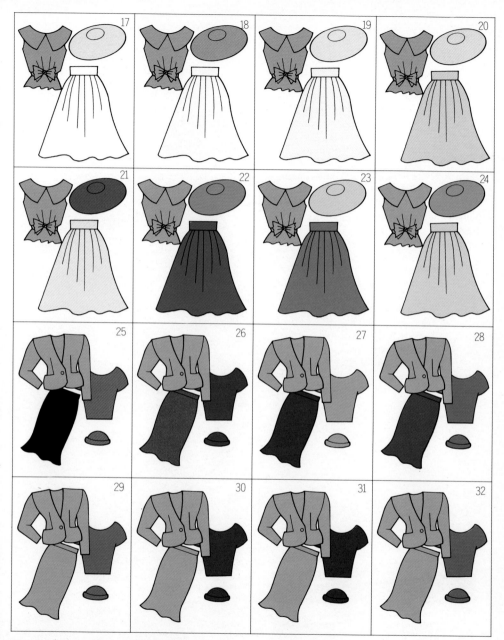

Light Purple—A Feminine Perogative

The lavender shown in 17-32 is based on violet. Combining lavender with light colors from the red family (18 and 20) gives a look of innocence and youth. Elegance and unity can be attained by matching lavender with other light colors of similar tonal value (21). As with light blue, if you choose dark or dull tones for the bottom part of an outfit (25-28), choose an accent color that will bring up the energy level of the outfit and keep it from falling flat. Dark colors that are close to black (30-31) can also be used with lavender to give a strong, conservative anchor.

Reddish Beige

From left: Cloudy pink / Plum gray / Pink beige / Beige

This group of light, grayish colors differ from monochromatic light gray because they also incorporate varying amounts of red. The stronger the red, the more vibrant the character of the color; conversely, the closer it is to the monochromatic, the less active and obvious it becomes. Although these colors give a weak impression by themselves, they can add stability and calmness to otherwise vibrant and cacophonous combinations. Because of their near-neutral tone, they are easy to coordinate with loud or insistent colors.

Reddish-beige can look heavy and lifeless if it is used in too dark a tone. Rose beige and soft pink harmonize with other colors without spoiling them. Though both are beige, there are slight nuances in each. Yellowish-beige feels more active and lively than beige with a straight reddish tone.

These natural hues can be used with a wide range of other colors and are an important basic building block for any large wardrobe. Used with dark colors, they become a bit masculine.

1
Reddish-beige is used as a base color, then dressed up with colors that are more insistent for a strong image.

2
When toned down, reddish-beige can become lifeless. Choose the secondary colors carefully.

3
Wearing a strong color with a tint of red will reinforce the red base of this beige.

4
The accents here are adjacent colors whose tonal values differ from the light beige base tone.

5
A light tint of taupe or sand, this beige is easier to coordinate with colors that have no common basis with red.

6
Used with dark beige, these tints will themselves look darker.

7
Use colors of different tones to vary the aspect of triadic combinations.

8
The common link in these colors is gray. A more active style to the clothing will keep it from looking flat or lifeless.

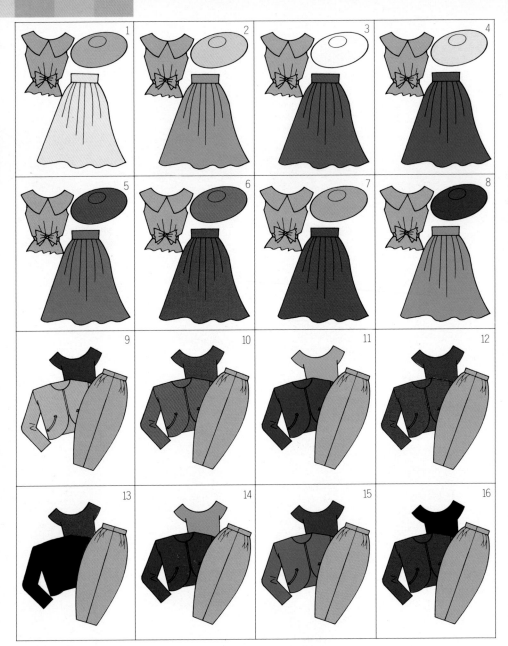

Dull Tones Of Pink Can Flatter Your Femininity

It will be very useful in building your wardrobe to find one basic color in this group that fits you well. Be careful in choosing, however, as some of these grayish tones may make you look melancholy, depending on your skin tone. Using a light grayish tone for a blouse or skirt brings calmness, warmth and mellowness to the combinations. While these shades are uninteresting when used as the color of a plain sweater, they work well as the base tone for a patterned one. The first 16 illustrations show a silvery pink made from red and gray. In 5-12, dark tones are used as secondary colors.

When using other deep colors (13-

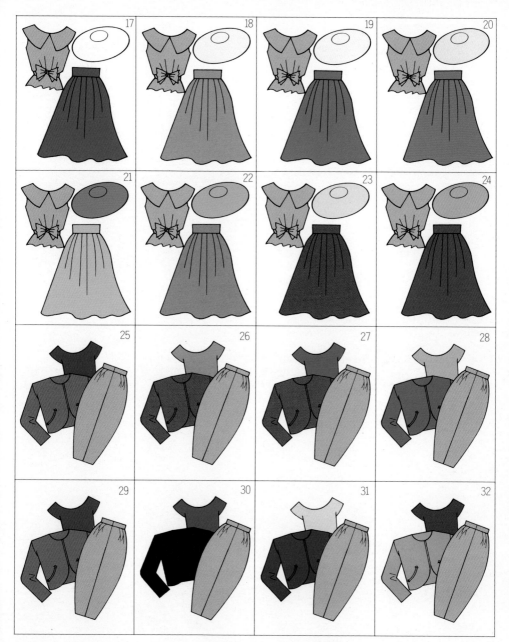

Yellow–Beige Fits The Classic Designs Well

16) put the beige at the bottom half of the outfit. The yellowish beige used in 17-32 is a more fashionable color than pink-beige. The colors used in 24 are all natural colors and blend together harmoniously. Very traditional tones are used in the combinations shown in illustrations 6, 19, 16 and 29. These color groupings will show classic styles of clothing to an excellent advantage. The beige keeps the outfits light while the deeper, grayed-down tones give them solidity and depth. The colors harmonize well and the overall result is calm and pleasing.

When gray is added to a group of vivid yellowish colors, they change to mild, simple colors. If the yellow is mixed with orange, the result is beige. But if the yellow has a bit of green, the resulting colors include various shades that are often called khaki.

Tan, camel and cinnamon are light brown colors related to these groups. Burnt sienna and yellow ocher are related earth colors.

Beige itself is a warm, whitish brown that is named for fresh-cut wool. It may also be called hemp, after the product of the hemp plant once used to make rope.

The various tones of yellowish-beige call to mind a host of images from nature. To add excitement, coordinate them with bright red, turquoise, emerald green or mauve. To reflect peace and project a quieter image, add dark blue, grape or mahogany.

These earth tones contain hints of yellow, green and gray. Although formerly used for casual wear, khaki, light brown and beige can be chic.

1

While utterly natural, this combination of blue-gray and beige looks very dry.

2

Adding secondary and accent colors in mild tones can dress up beige, making a fashionable impression.

3

A stronger impression can be made by adding deep tones, such as wine and navy blue.

4

Though understated, there are many fine and fashionable colors in this color family.

5

Try adding a vivid color to make beige more sporty. This pink looks both sporty and feminine.

6

The orange blouse gives the ensemble a bold look. The warm colors and contrasting tones make a jaunty statement.

7

These cool colors have, interest and complexity because all are of differing values and chroma.

8

The dark purple tone visually calms the overall impression made by this ensemble.

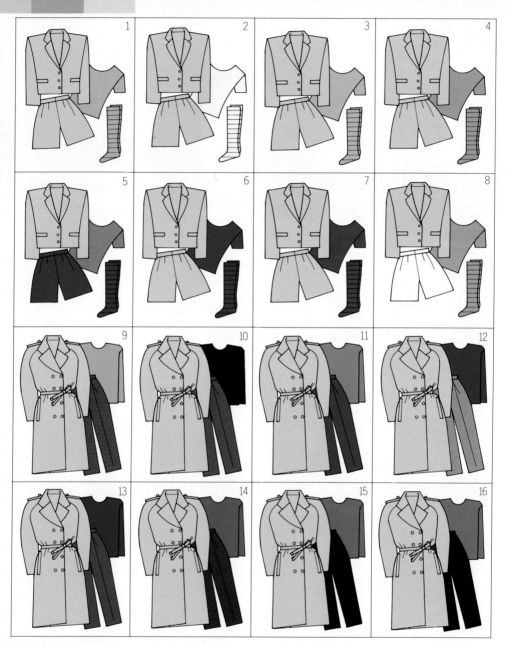

Beige Combines Elegantly With Many Tones

The beige used in 1-16 is made by creating a light tint of reddish-gray. While it mixes with other colors in much the same way as red, its lightness and the added gray widen the possible choices. Also, unlike tints of yellow, it works well on many types of fabric. Combine it with either lighter tones (1-4) for an innocent image, or with more vivid tones (5-8) to make a stronger impression. Quiet, dull tones are used in 9-12. The monochromatics added to 10 and 12 make them more masculine-looking. When combining beige with these dull colors, avoid using the darker shades of beige as they would make the groupings dark and brooding.

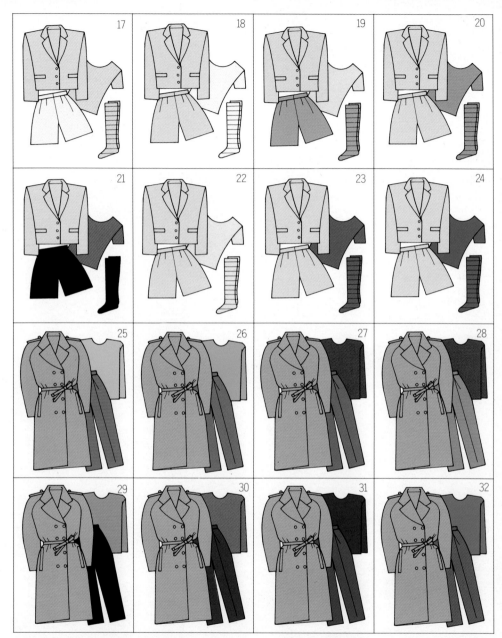

Beige: Romantic Or Trendy, Take Your Pick

The combinations illustrated in 17-32 are based on a more yellowish-beige. Compare it to the beige used in 1-16. It has a bit more individuality. If your goal is a light, romantic look, try the combinations shown in 17-20. The vivid colors used in 21-24 are brighter, and add a cheerful lift to the beige outfits shown. For a more stylish, elegant presentation, add two dull, grayish colors (25-28). A third color can be added as an accessory— something bright and vivid to provide a visual spark for the outfit. The colors in 29-32 are a little more fashionable, but choose them carefully so as not to unbalance the outfit.

Blue-Gray & Green-Gray

From left: Mist green / Mist blue / Blue gray

Quiet colors mixed with gray—misty, mossy, the color of water on a foggy morning. There is calmness and elegance in this color group. Adding yellow to the lightest green changes it to cactus; coordinating them with black as a point color will make them stylish and chic.

With the light green-gray, use secondary colors that are darker and warmer such as brown, khaki or a light olive color.

These colors give a different aspect and impression depending on your individual complexion, so compare them to your skin color carefully before wearing.

Because the gray comes through more strongly than the base colors in these shades, we can use them as a type of gray, combining with a wide variety of colors. They work well as a backdrop to more vivid colors.

1

Here's a way to combine green and purple without the slightest hint of brashness.

2

When you darken orange, it becomes brown. The low tone of this brown makes it harmonize well with green.

3

Red adds interest to a combination of high and low chroma greens.

4

These colors are adjacent, but interest is added by using shades with significant tonal differences.

5

A small amount of red-purple adds considerable punch and emphasis to this otherwise quiet combination.

6

Another group of adjacent colors with differing tonal values; use shades with strength to avoid a dull-looking outfit.

7

The chromas of these colors are all close together, but the bright colors give a fashionable feeling.

8

A very soft and quiet combination, this grouping is made of tones that are adjacent and have little tonal difference.

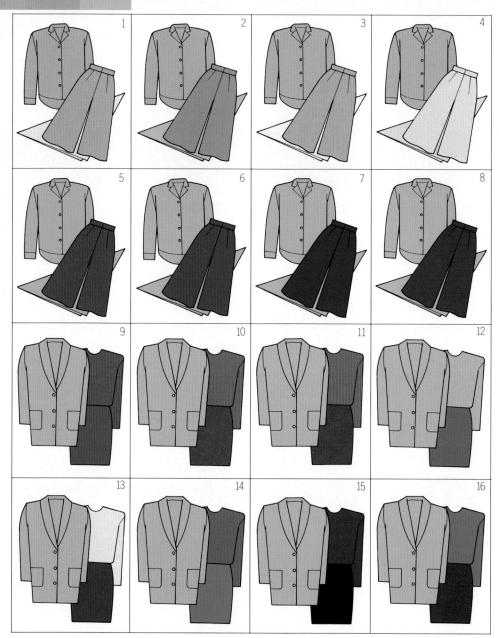

Mist-Green Combinations Show Style

Compared with beige, mist-green is a more sophisticated and refined color. It combines well with other subtle colors as opposed to bright, vivid ones. The grayish tones shown in illustrations 1-4 are a good example of soft tones that work well with mist-green. Light-colored accessories liven up the combinations. Darker tones (5-8) yield a stronger image, and monochromatic colors will help bring emphasis to these outfits. Groups including shades of red (9-12) make a more vivid statement, but are still calmed by the even, unruffled look of mist-green. Cool colors also work well (13-16); the greater the difference in tone, the better.

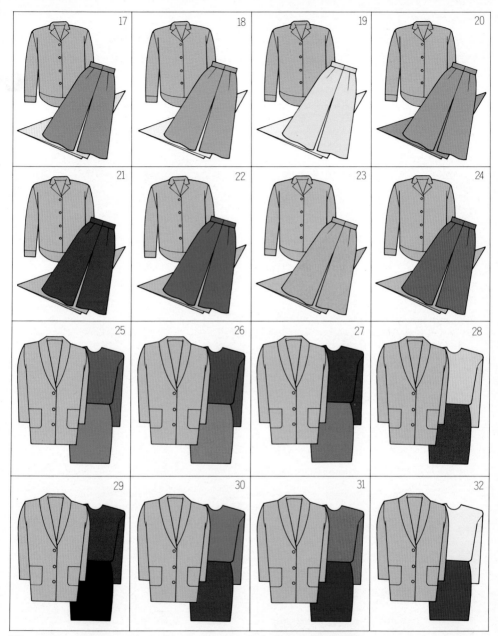

Use Blue-Gray For A Cool, Refreshing Feeling

Illustrations 17–32 use blue-gray rather than green-gray. When paired with tint colors (17–20), the result is cool and very calm. The purple tint (17) lends an air of quiet sophistication, while the green tints (18–19) are fresh and innocent. Used in a large enough quantity, blue-gray can lift the overall impression of an outfit that contains a predominance of dull, dark colors (25–28). More vivid tones of these colors are shown in illustrations 29–32. The high chroma of these colors provides a strong counterpoint to the lightness of the blue-gray.

Purplish Gray

From left: Smoke Blue / Lavender gray-blue
Light lavender gray/ Lavender gray-red

These delicate tones lie between violet and purple. Smoke blue looks like gray wood smoke drifting in the distance. The others are a bluish aqua-gray, purplish gray or silver gray and lavender gray.

All of these colors are weaker than full tints of their base colors, and can be used the same way that gray is used. Like beige, this makes a good base color for any wardrobe.

Because this group has a strong tinge of purple in the gray, combining it with monochromatics with high chroma makes a smart color scheme with a dressy feeling.

Pairing these colors with moderate tones such as dull colors or colors with similar tones creates a calm, pleasing harmony. To make them more lively, try adding yellow, which is the opposite of purple.

These light colors are between purple and violet, and retain a strong hint of blue. This shows the use of lavender gray with split complementaries.

1	2	3	4

Though this outfit combines cool colors with warm, harmony prevails because none have strong characteristics.

This split-complementary scheme looks fresh because it is unusual. Only a small amount of yellow is needed.

A variety of bright hues are integrated in this outfit. The light gray helps tie the colors together.

Here, red tones of differing strengths are used. Notice that the strongest tones are reserved for accessories.

5	6	7	8

The low degree of contrast between the tones of these colors helps them blend easily and naturally.

Though these colors are split complementaries, they blend well when the shades used have a low chroma.

Lavender-gray and navy blue fit well together. Introduce an opposing color, such as the olive used here, as an accent.

Here, peacock green makes a bright counterpoint to the light tints used for the jacket and skirt.

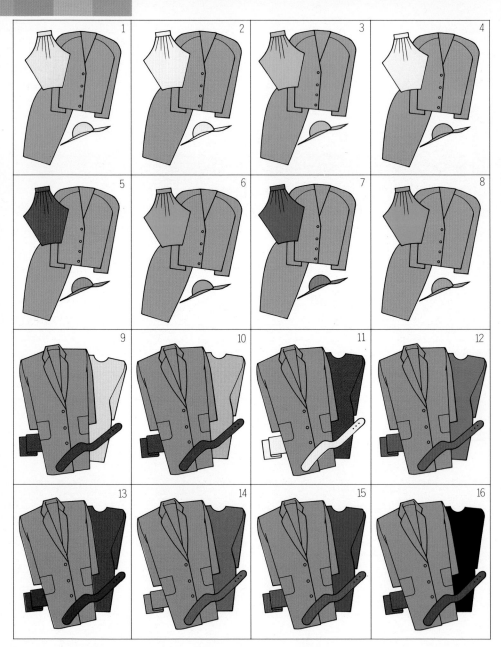

Use Contrasting Colors With Smoke Blue

Monochromatic gray is a good color; useful for many kinds of fabrics and ensembles. But when we change that gray, adding a hint of blue or purple, it becomes much more fashionable and mixes even more harmoniously with a wide range of colors. Using vivid colors (1-8) with smoke blue provides a visual punctuation mark to an otherwise dull outfit. Use the vivid colors as an accent, keeping their mass low, but choosing colors with high chroma. The combinations shown in illustrations 9-12 use dull tones of opposing colors, perfect for one-piece dresses and also useful for sportswear. While the colors are very different, the tones are close in value.

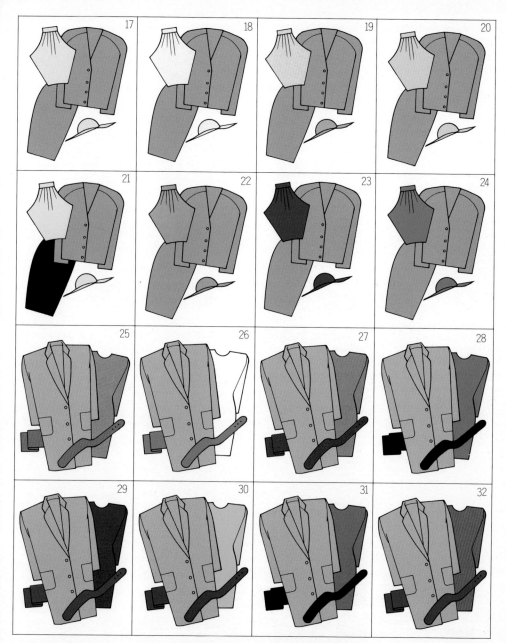

Lavender Gray For An Elegant, Adult Style

Using colors with a higher chroma (13-16) results in a more individualistic and pointed presentation. Number 14 uses opposing colors of different tones. The purplish tint of the grays used in 17-32 gives a more adult feeling to the outfits. When selecting secondary colors and accents, choose colors which are somewhat smoky, rather than clear, pure primaries. This will help the schemes blend together more readily.

The combinations shown in 25-28 show a variety of these tones. The combinations in 28 and 32 are especially delicate.

Deep Red Purple

Between red and purple on the color wheel lies a group of colors that typify wine and many kinds of dark berries. These colors keep the characteristics of both red and purple, exciting passion and fascination in equal measures. Deep red purple reminds us of a Nouveau Beaujolais, rich and full-flavored. Along with brown, this is one of the fall colors.

Raspberries, mulberries, plums, boysenberries and eggplants are among the fall crops that reflect this color group.

Using dark red purple with amber or black portrays a strong personality. Deep red purple reminds us of amethyst, which also belongs in this group. Combining this color with lavender gray or pale lilac makes for a gentle, feminine scheme. Combining it with deep grass green—an opposing color—will look cool and casual.

Deep red purple is a very chic color which looks elegant when combined with gray. Notice how the red tones of the blouse pick up and highlight the red in the jacket.

1

2

3

4

This scheme will be more active if the muffler is a contrasting tone; more harmonious if it's the same color as the skirt.

These colors have the same degree of tonal contrast as in 1. The addition of beige, however, adds warmth.

While the tones are similar in this grouping, the colors themselves are opposites, creating tension and visual interest.

Here, dark tones of opposing colors have been combined in a scheme that is harmonious and interesting.

5

6

7

8

Using clear colors from the same group tends to be a little too simple. Use different shades to highlight each color.

These light tones are from the same basic color group as in 5. Their lightness contrasts well with the dark jacket.

Tones of an opposing color, green, are used in a tonal scheme similar to that in illustration 2.

Stronger tones produce a more striking split-complementary grouping.

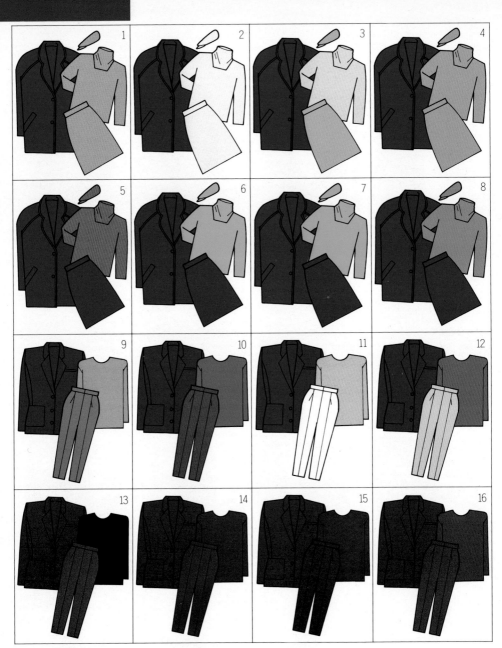

Deep Purple: Fashionable For Fall Wear

Deep purple can look sporty or masculine, depending on how it is used. The first four illustrations show combinations of purple with colors of different tonal values. These soft colors fit well in an urban setting. Adding a more vivid color (5-8) makes for a sporty look. The darkness of deep purple makes it a color with a lot of mass. The look of outfits made with deep purple can be lightened by adding a second and third color (9-12) in equal volumes. If you wear slacks and a shirt of the same color, try adding bright gold accessories. The dull tones illustrated in 13-16 work best when the colors are used in approximately equal volumes.

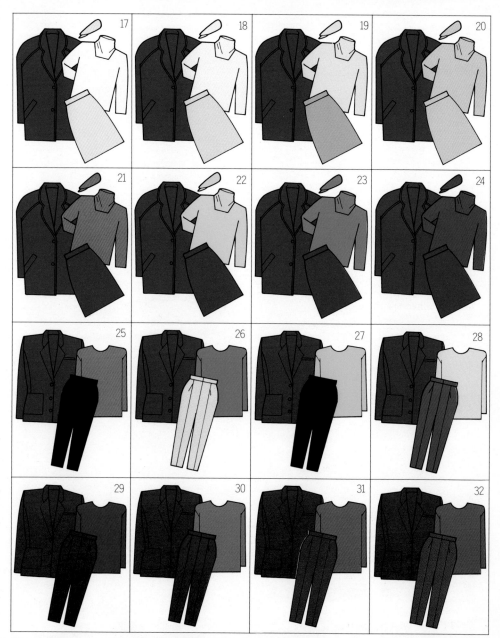

Red Purple: High Fashion Anytime

The deep red purple illustrated in 17-32 makes a more dramatic impression than deep purple. Still, by combining it with light tones, a sufficiently mild impression can be maintained. As with deep purple, adding colors with a higher chroma creates a more vivid and sporty image (21-24). The combinations shown in 27 and 28 use light tones of a cool color to create a soft and calm impression. Although the colors used in combinations 29-32 are dull, the image they project is hard-edged and chic.

Deep Wine

From left: Crimson / Garnet

Even red—the flaming, pyrotechnic segment of the color wheel—can look steady and gentle when it is worn in a deep shade.

Deep purplish red is a variety of crimson. When brown is added, it becomes garnet, very close to maroon. A bit darker and it becomes chocolate.

Use light tones of gray with these colors to keep them from becoming too heavy. A bluish steel gray will look chic while a yellow beige will look sporty; cinnamon or mustard will bring mildness.

Profound and warm, wine color wears well in winter with neutral tones of gold, olive or amber.

Using colors with similar values helps integrate dark red; adding contrasting tones, a light blue-gray creates a more interesting scheme. Try a bright blue or gold scarf as an accent.

1

Combining crimson with a bright rose color makes a well-coordinated but still interesting presentation.

2

An opposing color, green, in a shade with similar tone works when accessories, such as a scarf, tie them together.

3

The cream sweater and stripes on the skirt lighten this rich combination of similar tones.

4

Black provides a vivid counterpoint to the similar tones used in combination 1, freshening them.

5

Though blue and brown are opposing colors, they can be charming. A brown skirt would make the scheme harmonious.

6

These adjacent colors also have close tonal values. In this case, jewelry and accessories can be used to perk it up.

7

Using the heaviest color at the top upsets our sense of the ordinary. Note how the purple accent enlivens the group.

8

Bright tones of green, an opposing color, give a lively and sporty impression.

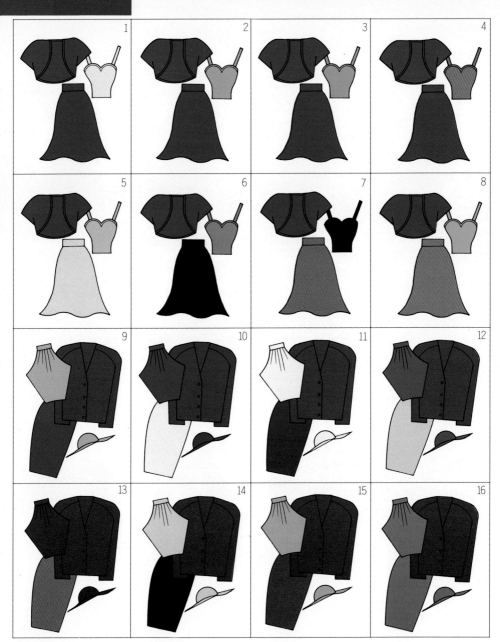

Bright Colors Update The Look Of Wine-color Garments

Deep wine colors have been used since the earliest times and they enjoy a classic aura. But you can update the impression they make by combining them with other, brighter colors. The combinations shown in 1-4 all share a common element of purple in varying shades. A wider variety of colors are shown in 5-8. The schemes shown in 9-12 are more daring, using opposing colors at the bottom of the outfits. Note that these tones are not vivid, but are a slightly dull shade to blend with the tonal value of deep wine. Combinations 13-16 are more elegant. Wear a silver brooch or emerald green earrings with the colors in 13, for example.

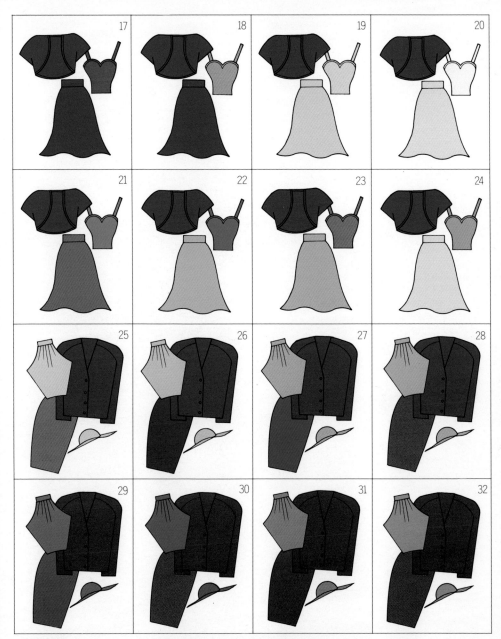

Reddish Brown Is Right For Sportswear

If crimson isn't quite your color, try the garnet shown in 17-20. For a more vivid look, try the bright colors shown in 21-24. If they seem a bit strong for your taste, try using them in small amounts as an accent on a scarf, belt or bag. For an altogether quieter combination, try one of those pictured in 25-28, where dull tones are used instead of the vivid ones. The clear tones of 25 are orthodox and look good on most people. Colors that are one step duller are pictured in 29-32.

Deep Red

From left: Cardinal red / Antique rose / Burnt orange

These colors call to mind the deep, viscous red seen on Japanese lacquerware. Exported to America and Western Europe in the 19th century, the brilliant finish and vivid colors of lacquerware became popular there, too.

The left-most color in this group, cardinal red, has been used since antiquity as a sign of dignity or high office. When this color is made a little darker, it becomes persimmon; a little darker yet and it becomes ox-blood.

This group works well as a color for a one-color suit or for a one-piece dress. Choose a similar color with light tones as an accent to project a gentle image, or add an opposing color with a similar tonal value or a dark tone to make a clean, strong presentation.

The low chroma keeps the otherwise aggressive colors in this outfit feeling gentle and feminine. The gray tones used for a scarf and shoes help tie the combination together.

1 Though both of these colors are reds, using the lighter shade tones down the flamboyant nature of high-chroma red.

2 Notice how the use of cardinal red, rather than vivid red, makes these opposing colors seem more harmonious.

3 Stripes, alternating cardinal red with beige, give a feeling of activity to the whole outfit.

4 Brown serves as a bridge between lavender and red, tying the two together in a fashionable combination.

5 This combination uses tint shades of similar, gray colors. Use ample volume of both and a different texture for each.

6 Here, a dull color is used with a clear, dark color. By choosing opposites —red and blue—a casual air is achieved.

7 Though the grayish color of this skirt looks a bit dull, it fits materials with a high nap very well and exudes warmth.

8 Here, brown and grayish green—opposites—are balanced nicely with a monochromatic (gray) skirt.

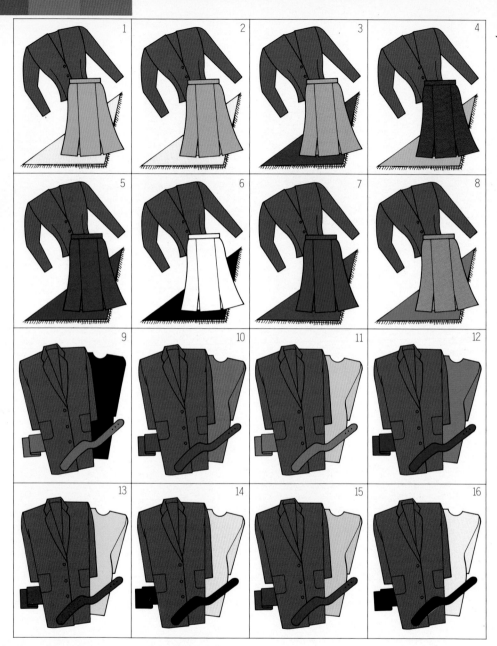

Cardinal Red Is Easy To Wear

Cardinal red works as a wardrobe color for men and women, so it suits popular unisexual clothing styles quite well. The color, though derived from red, can be thought of as a more vibrant shade of brown; in fact, its characteristics are very similar to those of the lighter browns. Illustrations 1-4 show how tint colors modify the brightness of cardinal red. Stronger colors (5-8) make a somewhat stronger, sportier impression.

The three-color combinations (9-12) weave together contrasting colors which are strong, though shown in dull tones, rather than vivid ones. The combinations in 13-16 have strong tonal contrast. When used

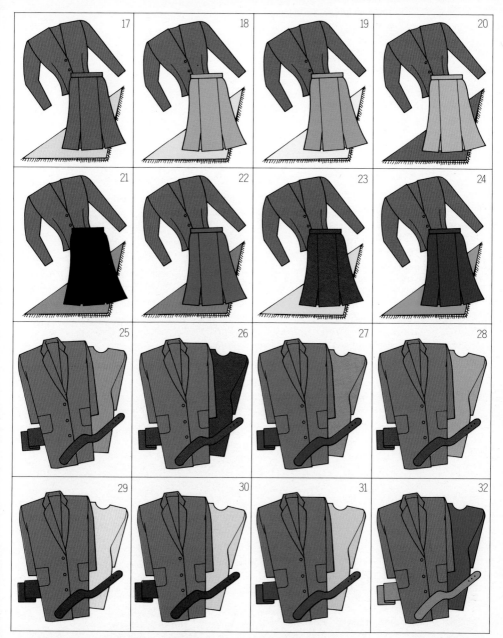

A Red That Fits Men & Women Well

with a light tint of red (14), the outfit can become a bit too sweet. Try adding a dark blue belt to deepen the look. Gray-green and gray-blue (18-19) match well with deep red. You could reverse the colors of the skirt and scarf shown in 21 to brighten the overall image. The quiet tones illustrated in 25-28 harmonize well, with no one element demanding attention. Number 26 can be ordinary looking, so use a dark color such as black or deep blue for the belt to spice it up. The combinations shown in 29 and 30 are very feminine; using purple accessories will accentuate the impression to the verge of being coquettish.

Deep Brown

From left: Maroon / Tobacco brown

These are profound, deep browns tinged with red or maroon. With a touch of yellow, they become mahogany brown or amber; with a little more red, they are called coconut brown.

Combining a thin, coffee brown gabardine suit with a salmon pink blouse is a way to show your fashion sense in late fall or winter. Replacing the blouse with a black sweater hints at originality, intellectualism and activity.

Because brown is so deep, it's important to combine it with colors in a way that avoids making your outfits look heavy. It fits well with bright colors, but darker tones of red or blue are apt to make a combination which is dull. To use red or blue, choose a lighter tint.

In temperate climates, a thin wool suit in brown bridges three seasons effortlessly. Simply change the colors of the accessories to make the outfit appropriate to the time of year.

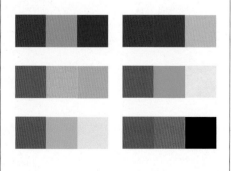

Three colors with low chroma are combined to make a sensible color scheme. Any one of the three could have been used as the main color without upsetting the balance.

112

1

This scheme uses split-complementary colors of similar tones. A stylish silhouette keeps these hues from looking dull.

2

This is a very simple coordination made by combining brown with a single color of similar tone.

3

Here, opposing colors are used for blouse and jacket. The tint of the skirt brightens the scheme and ties it together.

4

Here a bright color is added to a split-complementary combination to attract more attention.

5

A trendier shade of brown has been chosen for use with tints of split-complementary colors.

6

Here, the brown has been combined with a misty gray-blue; a very Japanese feeling ensues.

7

Here similar light tints of opposing colors make an active combination. The brown jacket quiets the ensemble.

8

Brown is not often worn with light blue, but when a light gray is added, the combination becomes harmonious.

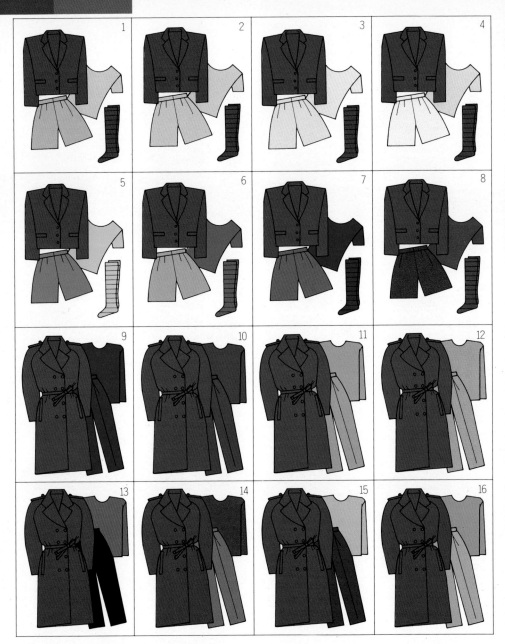

Maroon: A Wardrobe Basic

Maroon is a basic color that can be worn throughout the year. As such, it should be a staple in your wardrobe. It also combines well with a very wide range of other colors. Notice how light tint colors lift the appearance of the brown jacket shown in illustrations 1-4. These schemes are most appropriate for wear in early spring or fall. Although maroon and blue are opposites, they can blend well, as shown in 5- , whether the blue is light or dull. The vivid red added in number 8 makes a bold statement of independence. Though 9 and 10 are dark, the colors have strength. Light, grayish tones (11-12) make calm combinations that are nonetheless stylish.

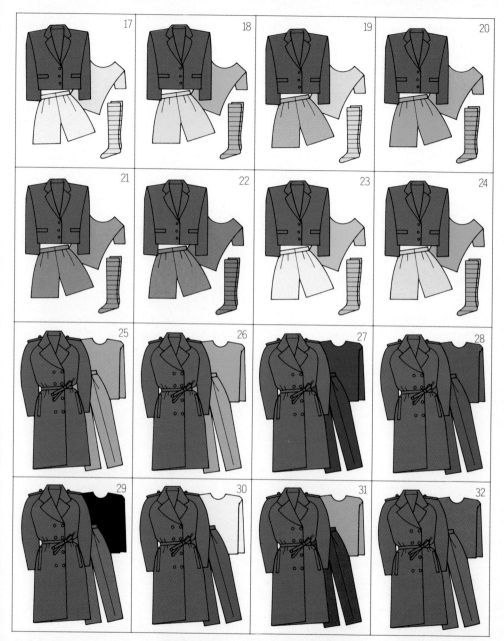

Add Accent Colors To Enliven Tobacco Brown

A high-chroma and low-chroma yellow are added to brown (1) to make it look fresh and active. By contrast, the light tones illustrated in 18 and 19 are very cool, but still fresh. While brown is ordinarily not a flamboyant color, using it with vivid tones, as in 21-24, makes very cheerful combinations. Keep the tones from getting too dark in this instance, or you'll be close to the rather masculine color schemes illustrated in 29-32. Neutral, grayish tones, as shown in the combinations illustrated in 25-28, have a very sober aspect. The tonal differences in 27 and 28 help add a bit of impact to otherwise lackluster combinations.

Light Brown

From left: Autumn leaf / Cinnamon / Ocher

Though brown generally has a very sober aspect, this group of colors has a remarkably light feeling. These browns are made from an orange that has been darkened so that it loses its vividness.

Autumn leaf is a sparkling brown. Its light tint color is amber; made slightly darker, it is copper.

Cinnamon is also called reddish-brown or bronze, while yellow ocher gives an impression of the earth.

These colors can be used as main theme colors in an outfit, or—because they combine well with other colors—introduced as an accent in many other schemes.

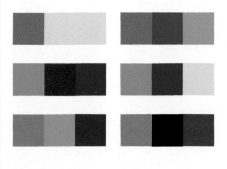

This scheme is chic for urban wear when coordinated with neutral, light tones of amber and bright—but low—tones of an opposing color such as blue. These strong colors will be shown to advantage if used on simple clothing.

1

Here, soft tones of adjacent colors make a soft combination. A darker bag or shoes will add depth to the scheme.

2

This is a grayer tone of the blue used on page 116, making the overall tone of the outfit much quieter.

3

This is a fashionable grouping that is at once casual and sporty. Clear beige will also work well for the skirt.

4

A stronger statement is achieved by pairing the orange-brown with purple and black. Wear gold accessories for elegance.

5

Yellow ocher can be a good foundation color for your fall wardrobe. Add a spot of reddish-brown to spice it up.

6

Here, a deep green tone is used to make this outfit more fashionable and to dress up the ocher.

7

This is a sophisticated, yet casual, scheme. To project a stronger image, try replacing the dull green with bottle green.

8

In this sophisticated color scheme, the burnt orange could be replaced with wine red, bottle green or deep blue.

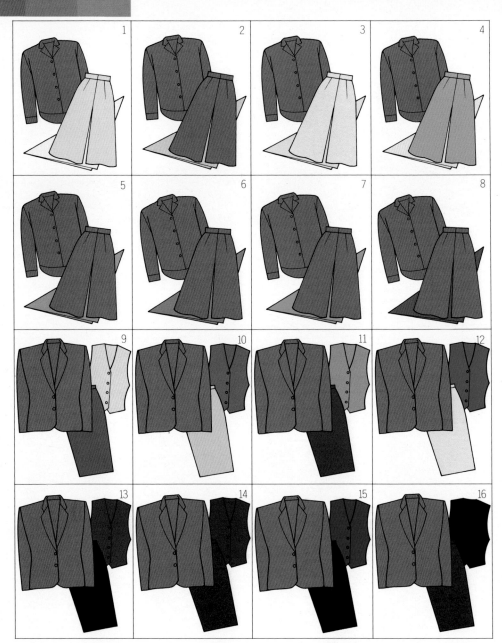

Combine Light And Grayish Tones With Light Brown

While light brown can be worn any time, choose the fabric of your outfits to match the feeling of the season. In spring or fall, consider cotton in light, tint colors. In fall, switch to wool, jacquard or tweeds of gray tones. A feeling of gaiety and youth prevails in the light tones illustrated in combinations 1-4. Vivid accents, a scarf or belt, bring brightness and color to the otherwise monotone schemes pictured in 5-8. The light-ness of brown combined with grayish tones makes it essential for suits (9-12). Using brown and purple togeth-er makes an especially warm combi-nation for late fall or early winter. The look is bright, fanciful and very

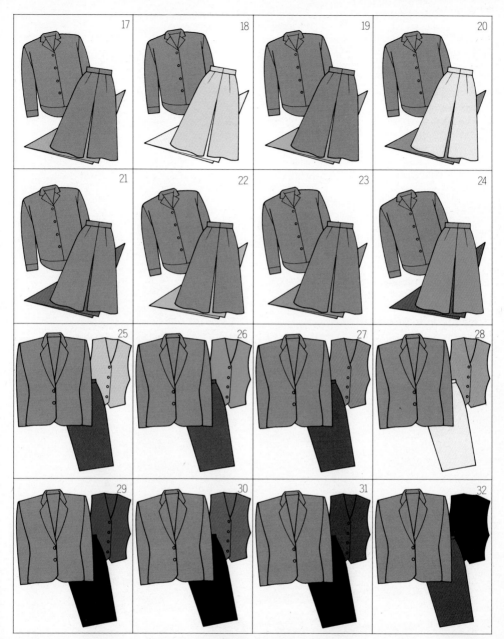

Ocher & Black: A Stunning Combination

pleasing to the eye. Try varying the proportions of the colors to create new and different effects. The dull tones in 14, 15 and 16 are very harmonious. You can use a shirt of one of the three colors under the vest and jacket. Yellow-ocher (17-32) also works with the same group of colors as light brown. While the light tones (17-20) are fresh and cheerful, try a little adventure by adding vivid tones, such as those illustrated in combinations 21 and 24. Notice how the ocher tones down the bright pink vest (27). By using black as one of your main colors (29-32) you will be able to combine ocher with a wide range of dull tones.

Dark Yellow
From left: Gold / Olive

Here, yellow has been combined with other colors to make darker, more complex tones. If red is added, a gold color results. If even more red is added, the color becomes golden brown. If the yellow is tinted with blue, it becomes a sober-looking color such as mustard yellow.

Khaki, which is well known as a military color, is part of this group. Light khaki was adopted by armies as a camouflage, to make troops blend with natural surroundings. In your wardrobe, it can blend with its surroundings as well, setting off other colors to good advantage. It plays the same role as monochromatics, adding delicate nuance to your color schemes.

Khaki and other brownish yellows have been very popular in recent years. Combining them with bright blue makes a conspicuous, but harmonious, outfit. The look is hard and sharp, and gives an impression of youth.

1. Amber is used to accent two shades of gold. The difference in tones makes for a casual look.

2. A purple accent adds elegance to this combination of non-descript colors. Bright red would show a youthful aspect.

3. Adjacent colors with differing tonal values make this group work. This scheme would also perk up military-style clothes.

4. This cool-looking combination uses deep green to give vibrancy to the gold color. Dark brown slacks would add depth.

5. The hard-looking, military tones of this outfit are brightened and softened by the use of cream yellow.

6. Here, an orange and an olive of similar tonal values present a strong contrasting scheme.

7. Wearing a light tint of yellow-green with olive, then adding a gray of similar tonal value, projects a stylish image.

8. Olive combines naturally with this secondary color. The two can be balanced with dark brown.

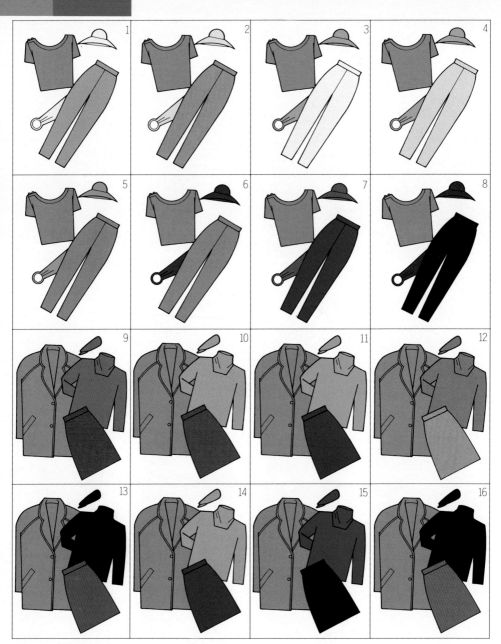

Gold Highlights Other Colors

Gold is neither dark, nor heavy, nor conspicuous, but it brings other colors into prominence and is very easy to use. The combinations of gold and grayish tones (1-4) are soft and refined. Using a deeper, more profound color (5-8) highlights them. Darker grayish tones (9-12) are tasteful, if a bit more somber than the lighter tones shown in 1-4. The tones in 12 are especially tasteful, and note how the monochromatic gray is used to brighten the grouping. Black and dark colors (13-16) look very good with gold. They give solidity to the color schemes and provide a vivid anchor, especially when used at the bottom of an outfit.

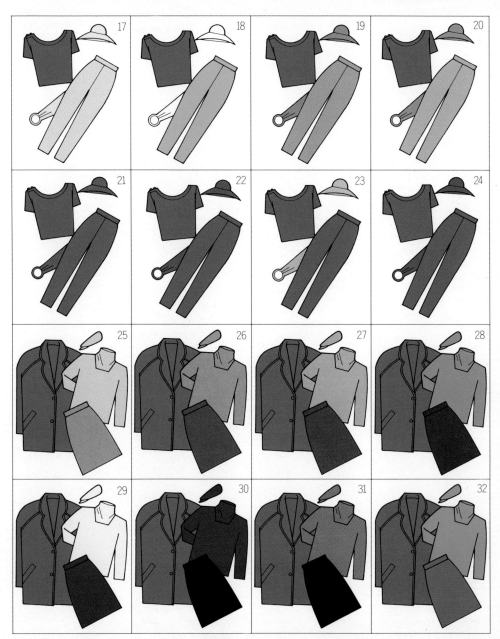

Be Bold With Olive And Vivid Tones

As with gold, light tones used with olive are fresh-looking and are appropriate for wear in the spring and summer, when the sun is shining and flowers are blooming. Vivid colors make a bolder statement (21-24), but still give an impression of freshness. In these cases, use a sufficient volume of olive so that it remains the main or theme color of the outfit. While 23 shows olive with an adjacent color, the scheme in 24 shows split complementaries. Olive green can look very stylish when used with a tint of green and a monochromatic (25), while darker tones (26-28) present a more sober aspect that wears well in the fall and into early winter.

Dark Green
From left: Oil yellow / Moss green / Olive green

These greens are a little yellowish and are slightly dull—gray has been added to them. When vivid yellow green is darkened, it results in a very sober color, such as an olive tinged with both brown and green. This is a natural color; present in nature in many guises—willow bark, moss, grass, and of course the leaves of the olive tree.

Adjacent colors like gold, golden brown and beige are a natural complement to olive green, while bright or tint shades from opposite colors make a more profound and vivid impression.

Olive green creates warmth when used with quiet, gray tones such as these. When used with a darker, more saturated tone, it becomes a calming influence, smoothing the impression of strong colors.

1

Here, adjacent colors are used with olive. When wearing them together, use colors with similar tonal values.

2

Here, the usual roles of color are reversed. The lighter color is quieter and the darker color has become the focus.

3

When using adjacent colors that contrast, such as this cool blue-green, use black or another dark color as an accent.

4

Medium gray evens out the tonal values of this scheme and keeps it from becoming too flamboyant.

5

Here, similar colors of different tones are used together. As an accent, choose black or another dark color.

6

Notice how the midnight blue shirt—ordinarily a dull, sober color—sparks these similar colors and provides a bright focus.

7

Differences in color are conspicuous. It can be made more mature by reversing the colors of the skirt and the sweater.

8

Try replacing the blue shown in 6 with a bright orange color, as illustrated here.

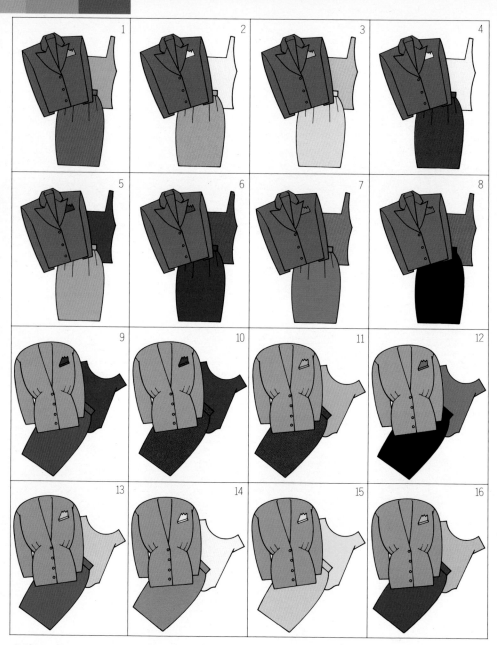

Olive Green Matches Dark Brown

Olive green has complex nuances and can be both sporty and masculine. When using it with a light color, use a lesser volume of the light color. While the scheme illustrated in 1 is a fine combination, all of these are sober, bitter-looking colors. A dark brown or black bag and brick-colored shoes would soften the impression. Combinations such as 2 and 3 work better when the amount of light color used is smaller. By changing the main color from olive green to yellow-green, the colors will look less gray. Therefore, even dull shades can be used with it (9-12). The schemes in 12-16 are flexible; the colors of the skirt and jacket can be reversed.

126

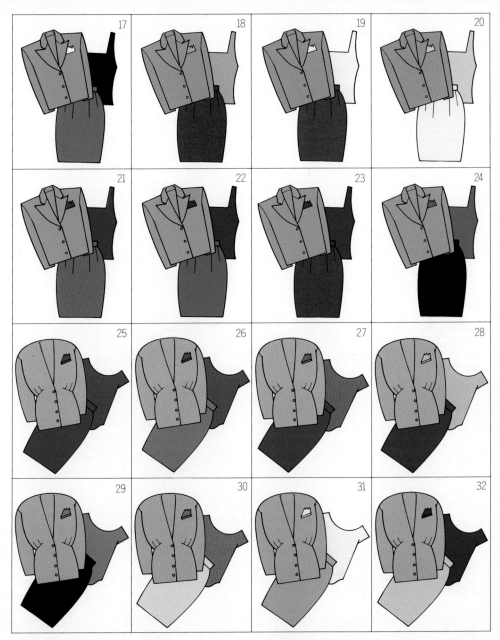

Dark Yellow-Green Is Tasteful Yet Cheerful

The color combinations illustrated in 17-20 are made with adjacent colors and show a nice harmony. In 21-24, adjacent colors are used, but there are more substantial differences in tone. This makes a stronger state-ment but the combinations are still very easy to wear. Number 24, in particular, has a very fashionable flair, while 21 and 22 are somewhat masculine in appearance. Dull, rather than clear, colors are used in combinations 25-28. Here, the gray acts to tie together the various shades. Like 24, 29 can be very chic, but its basic impression is strong and vibrant despite the dull tone of blue used for the blouse and pocket square.

Deep Green

From left: Evergreen / Viridian / Bottle green

The colors in this group could all be found in a an evergreen forest: The shiny, effervescent yellow-green seen in the young needles of pine trees; the bluish green of fir; and the dark bottle green of mature Scotch pine.

The yellow-green in this group is called evergreen. Dark blue-green is malachite—a mineral color—while lightening it slightly makes viridian. And the darkest color of this group, bottle green, is named for the color of the darkest glass used to make wine bottles.

A grouping of clear, dark greens like bottle green creates a sense of calm. Adding colors which fall between orange and red-purple on the color wheel adds depth to them. Use these colors alone to be sporty or casual, or dress them up in outfits with gold or silver sequin accessories.

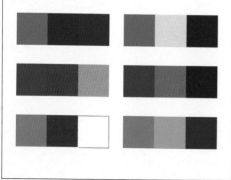

Here, the coolness of the colors moderates the flamboyant combination of green and purple. The result is youthful and intelligent. For a softer impression, substitute a beige blouse.

1

Here, clear green is used with grayish tones; greenish-gray for the slacks and grayish-brown for the shirt.

2

The deep, strong tones of the darker greens work well when paired with khaki or beige.

3

Using a check pattern with a lighter accent color helps brighten the otherwise heavy nature of dark green.

4

A difference in tonal values makes this a bright scheme. Try replacing the pink shirt with beige for less flamboyance.

5

This outfit would work well in winter. The beige pants add a cold-weather twist to the basic combination of green and red.

6

Here, a more purplish tone of red is used to add flamboyance to the outfit. Deep red would not be nearly as fashionable.

7

Beige skirts almost beg to be paired with a blazer of a dark, clear color, such as this green.

8

The differences in tone and color make this a strong grouping. Try these colors in patterns with checks or stripes.

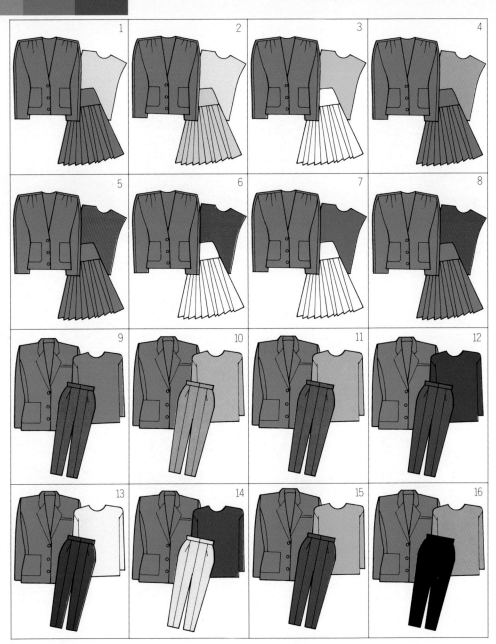

Deep Green Creates A Sense Of Calm

Green has the same tonal value as medium gray, so it is by itself neither a dark nor a light color. This makes it easy to use green with both dark and light colors. The combinations shown in 1-4 are crisp and fresh, their appearance kept lively by the use of light tints. A stronger, more mature image is projected by the combination shown in 5, where a small amount of magenta sets a strident tone for the outfit. Though the colors in 6 are opposites, you can bring them together gracefully by using a tartan plaid pattern. The groupings shown in 9-12 make good schemes for business clothes. Large tonal differences (13-16) make outfits look

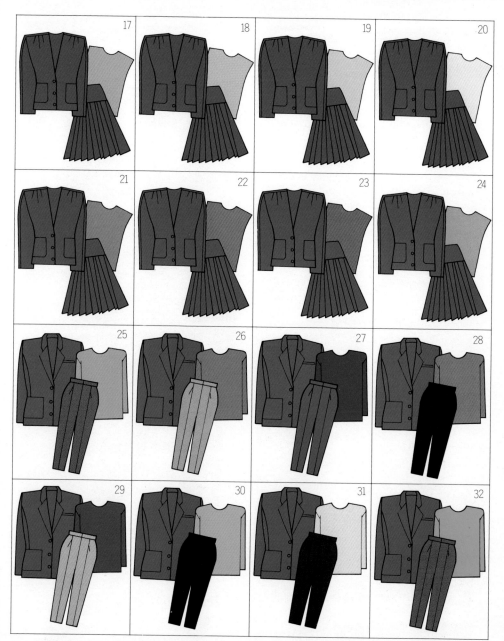

Bottle Green And Gray Tones: Instant Sophistication

very sharp. If you use only a small amount of color like bright pink (16), the weight of green will be enough to soften the outfit by itself without adding dull tones. Lighter tints of these colors (17-20) are more subdued and don't need to be softened. Using green with orange, red or purplish-red (21-24) will create conspicuous combinations, but again, the deepness of the green can prevent them from being too loud or overbearing. Use dull tones (29-30) sparingly with green. More vivid colors (31-32) give a spark to these dark green shades.

Deep Blue

From left: Blue-green / Gray-blue / Marine blue

Blue is the mysterious color of a deep pool or a boundless expanse of ocean. It gives a sense of space and quietude. A deep, clear blue is called marine blue; deeper still, and it becomes majolica blue, a dark tone used with white on Spanish and South American glazed pottery. Indigo is a deep, purplish-blue, such as that used on blue jeans. Navy blue is taken from the deep blue worn by English seamen for several centuries.

There are many subtle shades of these colors, ranging from deep and iridescent to dull and gray. All of them have been used widely for clothing and have become a traditional mainstay of many wardrobes.

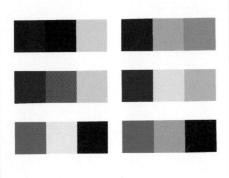

Deep blue is easy to use, combining with many colors quietly and naturally. Notice how a light tone, tea green, is used to soften the tension created by the dark blue and reddish-brown in the above ensemble.

1

Differing shades make a dramatic combination. Adding peacock green to these various blues gives them an obvious spark.

2

Here, brown is used to warm up the overwhelming coolness of deep blue.

3

The cool nature of blue can be used to good advantage. Here, it is used to calm down the flamboyance of orange.

4

An orangish-beige gives warmth to this outfit while the light yellow-green jacket adds a sense of fashion.

5

A series of light tones, all of them slightly gray, can be used together to create a bright impression.

6

Grayish blue also combines well with maroon, red-brown and cocoa.

7

Using too many dark tones is apt to dull the impression of grayish-blue, so add a clear blue color to highlight it.

8

Similar colors with differing tonal values are used for skirt and jacket, softening the brightness of the beige blouse.

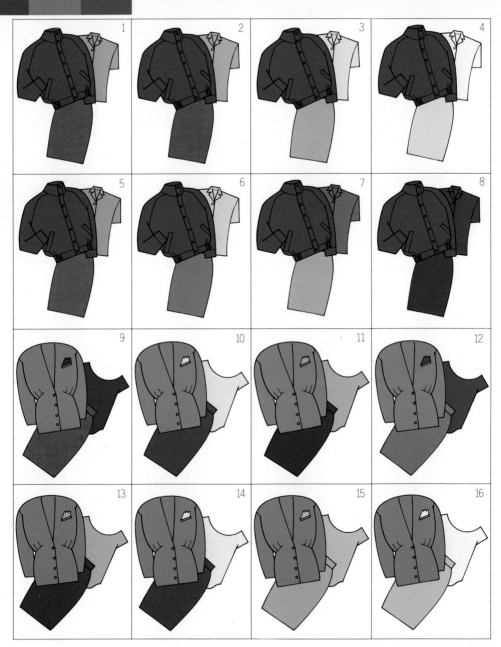

Deep Blue For A Masculine Edge

While deep blue is a traditional shade, it can also have a lively and fashionable application in your wardrobe. The deep, hard tones of the blues used in groupings 1–8 can be warmed up by simply adding brown or reddish-brown tones. Notice how the various shades of brown used in 2, 3 and 7 brighten the overall look of the outfits. A softer blue is shown in 9–16. While still very cool in visual temperature, it is far less insistent than the deep blue above. As with the darker shades, try pairing this lighter blue with various tones of brown and red—the purplish color in 9, the midnight blue in 13, or even the burnt-orange in 14.

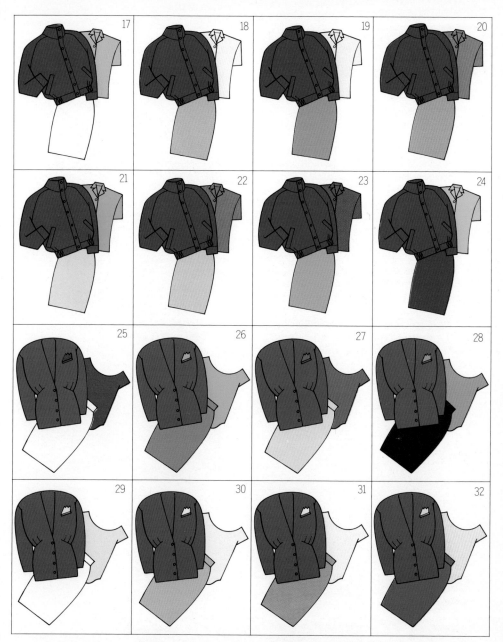

Lively Schemes Can Also Be Made With Deep Blue

For a livelier impression, choose secondary colors that are clear or tint shades rather than gray or dull. This will not only make the groupings appear fresher, but more feminine as well. An orange brown (22), looks better than dull brown alone, although a tint of brown, as seen in this skirt, works nicely with deep blue. The color combinations illustrated in the groupings numbered 25-32 use a brighter, marine blue as the predominant color, and it dominates even the tricolor arrangement pictured in 25. For a stronger image, use the vivid colors; to play down the colors of the outfits, try tint shades as shown in illustrations 29-32.

Deep Blue-Purple

From left: Orient blue / Royal blue / Aubergine / Navy

The addition of a small amount of purple can help warm up deep blue. It is the color of dark satsuma-kiriko glass produced in Kagoshima Prefecture in Japan. It is also royal blue, long used by the royal family of Great Britain, and seems appropriately majestic for a kingdom surrounded by the sea.

If more purple is added, the color becomes violet, a bright floral shade. Add black to this color and it becomes grape; add more and the grape becomes the color of concord grapes.

Deep blue is one of a group of colors that are called purple navy, which is different from navy blue. Using it with a reddish-purple makes a fascinating contrast. To create more tension, use it with opposing colors between orange and green and with dull tones of grayish colors.

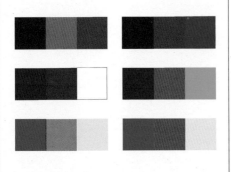

Purple, deep red and deep orange are all fully-saturated colors. Combining them makes a vivid and rich impression, especially if a high-nap or embroidered material is used. Wear a gold accessory or create an exotic mood by adding turquoise blue.

 1	 2	 3	 4
Combined with shades of rose pink, royal blue becomes innocent, evoking the image of a young girl.	Cream and purplish-gray are used with royal blue to project a more mature mood.	When using beige with royal blue, an accessory of burnt orange helps add a note of cheerfulness.	A vivid color, such as this clear green, makes this grouping very bright, appropriate for wear in early summer.
 5	 6	 7	 8
Reddish purple can be used to perk up an otherwise dark combination, such as aubergine and olive.	A flamboyant combination can be toned down by simply varying the intensity of the tones used.	This grouping has the same difference in tonal values as that in number 6 but the colors are more saturated.	If dark blue is used instead of aubergine, the result will look harder and more masculine.

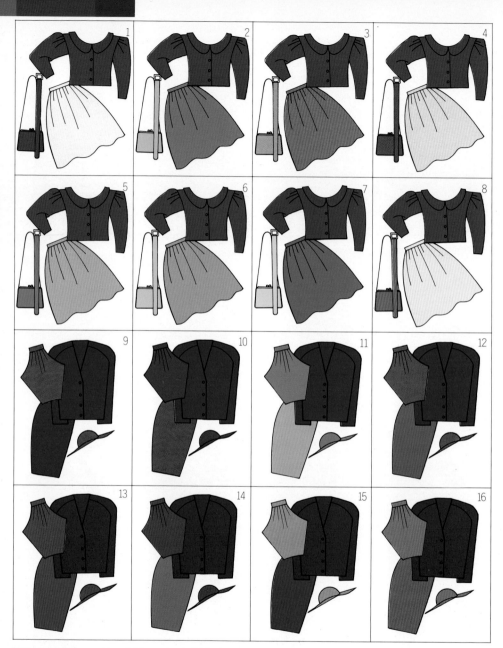

Bluish Purple Allows A Wide Range Of Combinations

This bluish-purple is rarely encountered in nature, so it has a strong visual impact. Because it is not overly bright, it can be combined with a multitude of tones and shades. The color combinations illustrated in groupings 1-4 are made with tint shades as secondary colors and grayish tones for the accessories. The outfits are appropriate for spring or summer. Be careful to use the heavy blue-purple at the top in small volumes so as not to overpower the tint colors. A monochromatic green works well with bluish-purple (5-7). To lighten the look, try the combination in 8, or reverse the colors of the skirt and accessories for an even brighter

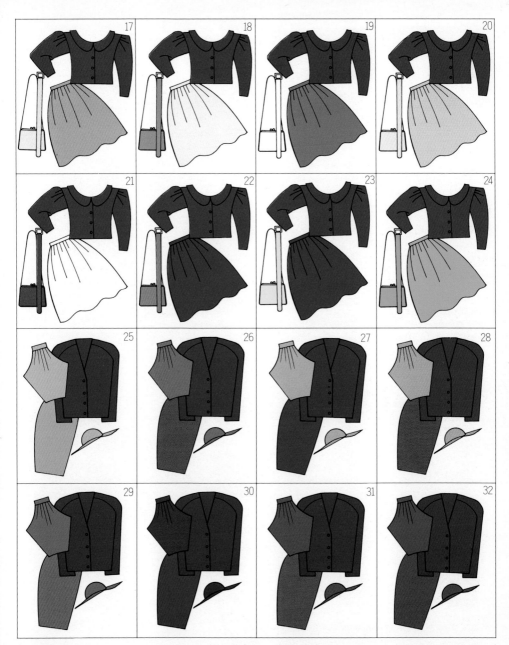

Contrasting Accessories Bring Out The Vibrancy Of Deep Purple

effect. The greenish gray in 9-12 is aubergine, a color with a long tradition in Japan. Using clear colors (17-24) brings out the most interesting characteristics of both the theme color and the secondary color. It is safe to use accessories which show a small volume of the accent color as in illustration 23, because this deep blue-purple makes such an excellent contrast. A softer, duller color makes somewhat safer combinations (25-32). The dullness of the color makes it a bit harder, so the combinations shown in illustrations 29-32 are most suited to adults in somewhat formal situations rather than sportswear.

Deep Purple
From left: Royal purple / Raspberry red / Grape

Like other colors, the mood of purple can be modified by using it with other colors. But its basic nature always seems to surface: elegant, passionate, mysterious.

Royal purple got its name because the dye used to make it in ancient times was so expensive. At that time, a Mediterranean shellfish was the only source of the dye, and it took up to 2,000 of them to produce one gram of pigment. Trading in this pigment was one of the fundamental pillars of the vast sea-trade of the Phoenicians, the ancient world's most adventurous mariners.

Today, purple can be made from synthetic dyes. And as new synthetic dyes have been invented, the brightness of the purple colors they create has increased. The tones of the color available for use on fabric may have changed, but the image it creates has not—our choices in how we use it have simply increased. Add olive brown to make a modern statement, or go classical with antique rose or lavender gray.

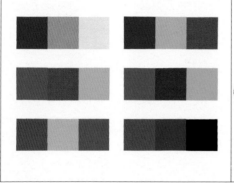

Using bright, clear colors with purple makes a very strong image. Using softer tones, as above, creates a more feminine look. The antique rose blouse paired with a smartly-tailored suit projects an image of simplicity and elegance.

140

1 Similar tones of blue colors are combined in this grouping. Use a maroon bag or shoes to create a classic mood.

2 Adding light gray-green and olive create an austere elegant look.

3 Adding a light tone to these otherwise somber shades brightens this outfit and makes it look more casual.

4 Dark brown adds depth to this scheme, helped by the use of a mustard yellow accent. This is fashionable and sporty.

5 Use bright red-purple with ivory or sand-gray to make a light, neutral and sporty combination.

6 Here, two purples are combined. The darker skirt helps tone down the brightness of the blouse.

7 A small touch of grayish-blue helps cool off the otherwise overwhelming impression of this vivid purple.

8 Here, a darker tone of gray-blue is added to red-purple to accentuate, rather than diminish, the passion of red-purple.

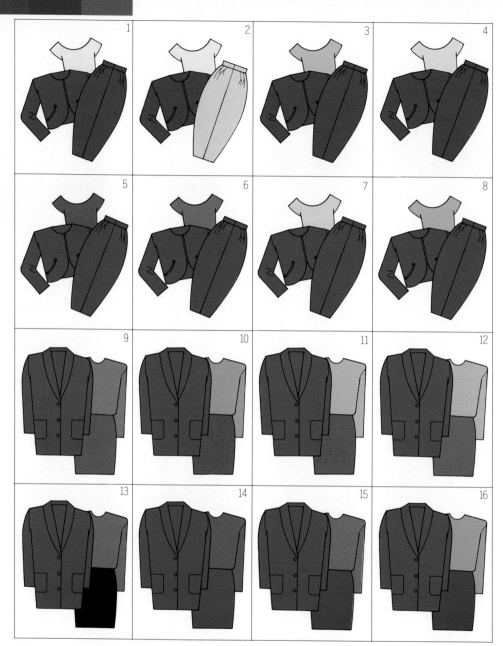

Use Royal Purple For Elegance

Don't let the flamboyance of this group of colors unnerve you: If you aren't comfortable wearing them with bright vivid colors that accentuate their flamboyance, then wear them with dull tones of brown or blue. The light, soft colors of 1-4 give a clear impression and are very flattering to young people with fair complexions. The reddish-purple used in 2 has a hint of red, brought out by the soft pink. The grouping shown in illustration 3 is good on people with well-defined features. One of the most useful characteristics of purple is its ability to hold its own when paired with strong colors, such as those shown in 5 and 8. Wear them at

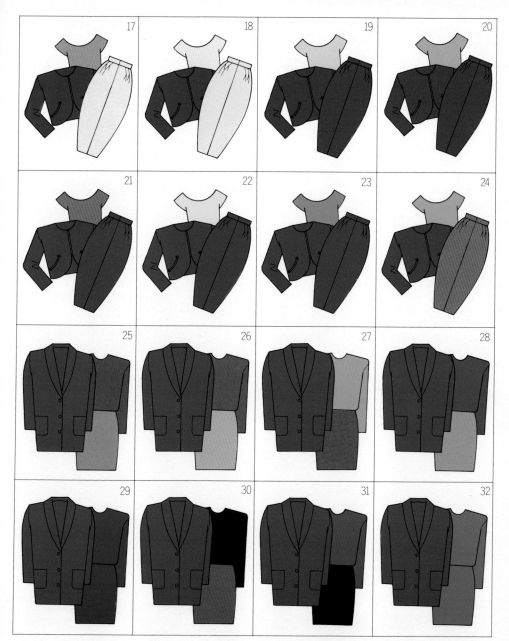

Red-Purple: A Passionate Match For Brown And Blue

resort areas, or on midsummer sports outings. The dull colors shown in 9-12 scale down the impression made by the purple. If you wear a dark color at the bottom of a purple outfit (13, 16), the result is elegant. The colors in 15 would work well in a large pattern. The red-purple in 17-32 is sometimes called raspberry red. It's a bit more daring than the other purples in this group. When making three-color combinations with rasp-berry red, it can act as a bridge, unifying the other two tones. The three colors in 24 would also make an admirable patterned fabric. A simple two-color combination, such as 32, makes a gentle, mature statement.

Dark Gray 1
From left: Gray-brown / Sea pine / Gray-green

The dull gray colors in this group are all tinged with a slight hint of earth colors: brown and green, as shown above, or with red, blue and yellow.

Adding red to this group will give you the plum gray which has traditionally been very popular in Japan. All are dull gray and are classified as either deep or soft depending on their tonal value. These colors can be seen in the ukiyoe wood-block prints of scenes from Japan's Edo period. The style and colors used in these block prints became fashionable in the West after they were adapted by popular artists such as Patrick Nagel and Robert Blue.

In general, combinations made with them are sober and adult, rather than flashy or adventurous. They have become traditional and classic, so their use is not likely to be greatly affected by trends that raise and lower the popularity of the more trendy colors.

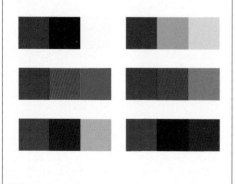

Gray-brown has the best characteristics of both gray and brown: It presents a certain warmth, as does brown, and it harmonizes effortlessly with a wide range of other colors.

 1	 2	 3	 4
Combined with garnet, grayish brown looks very rich, almost velvety. This is a traditional combination for winter clothes.	Different shades of gray-brown can be used together. Add green-gray, as in the blouse, to freshen its appearance.	To liven up the look of gray-brown, try adding a bright accent of mustard yellow.	Deep blue makes a casual match for grayish brown. Notice how the green shirt brightens the entire outfit.
 5	 6	 7	 8
This combination is not particularly harmonious. Adding a black belt or other accessories will give it some unity.	Here, similar colors of widely different tones are used together. Add warmth by wearing a brown-toned accessory.	Here, red-purple is used as the focal point of a split-complementary grouping. Gray-green keeps the outfit calm.	Using a tone of red introduces an opposite color. Choose an accessory that ties together the colors in the grouping.

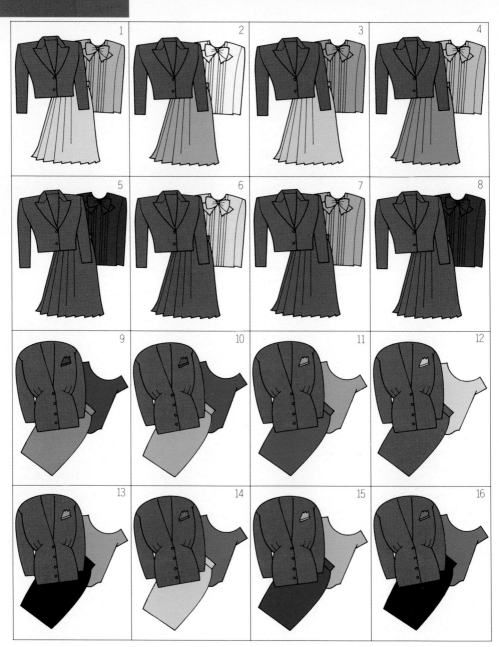

Use Light Tints With Grayish Brown

Although monochromatic gray is very easy to coordinate, when tinted with another color, its uses expand and become more complex. This is especially true when you use dull colors with the gray tints. The groupings illustrated in 1-16 are of a gray that is slightly tinted with orange. Use a mild color when combining this tone. Notice how a deep red, as shown in illustration 5, looks tasteful without attracting attention when paired with grayish brown. The wine red used in 8 looks all the more bright by being paired with grayish brown. A variety of tonal values are used for the inner clothes pictured in illustrations 9-12, while the groupings shown in 13-16

146

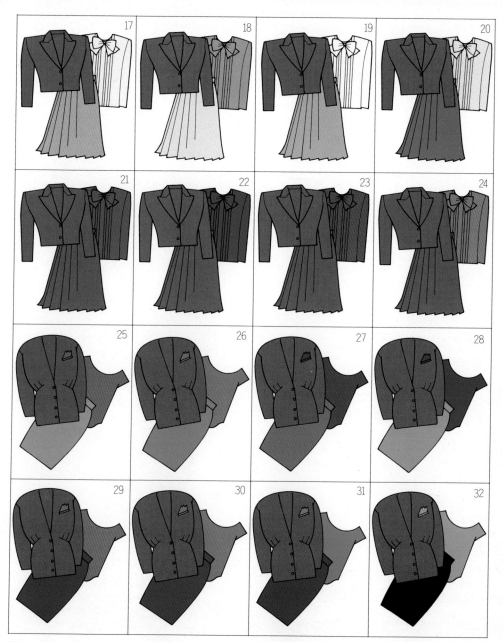

Try Bright Colors To Spice Up The Grays

are a little bit toned down. The low contrast and cool colors of 13–15 make these combinations a bit hard and cool. The bright pink used in 16 helps lighten the overall look of the outfit, but its purplish cast gives it a cool flavor rather than the warmth you might expect from a more vivid red. The dull green gray pictured in illustrations 17–24 can be lightened by choosing orange, an opposing color, as its secondary (24). Yellowish-gray (25–32) also works well with low tones of brown, blue and green. A dark green skirt (30) and yellow-gray jacket can be tied together and livened up by the use of a burnt-orange blouse.

Dark Gray 2

These colors are generally modest and unassuming. But they work gracefully with many other colors and, with bright accents, can be quite fashionable.

Opposing colors, in particular, help heighten the sense of fashion.

Be careful when combining these colors; if used with other dull tones, your outfits will be lusterless and monotonous. Vary the tonal value of the colors you use to combine with these shades. Make them lighter or darker, even black.

The muted quality of this group is excellent for creating a neutral, but stylish, backdrop for your favorite scarf, hat or jewelry.

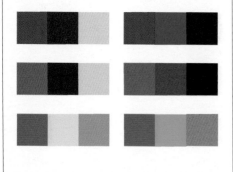

Both gray and purple gray are quiet colors. Here, purple gray is combined with deep green for a mature, but vivid, impression. If monochromatic gray is substituted, the result will be masculine.

1

2

3

4

When using light tones, such as this blouse and skirt, try adding a dark belt to give the outfit focus.

In this illustration, brown tones have been used to add warmth and depth to the combination.

Three colors with different tones are combined. The dark purple is the darkest, gray the lightest and green is a mid-tone.

Harmonious colors with tonal differences give a feeling of high fashion and refinement to this combination.

5

6

7

8

Beige is used to lighten the overall appearance of this split-complementary scheme.

Here, the colors are of different values, but all have a common element—a slight hint of red.

These saturated tones also work well for knitted sweaters and other high-nap materials.

This split-complementary scheme is held together by a large volume of black, making a typical Japanese grouping.

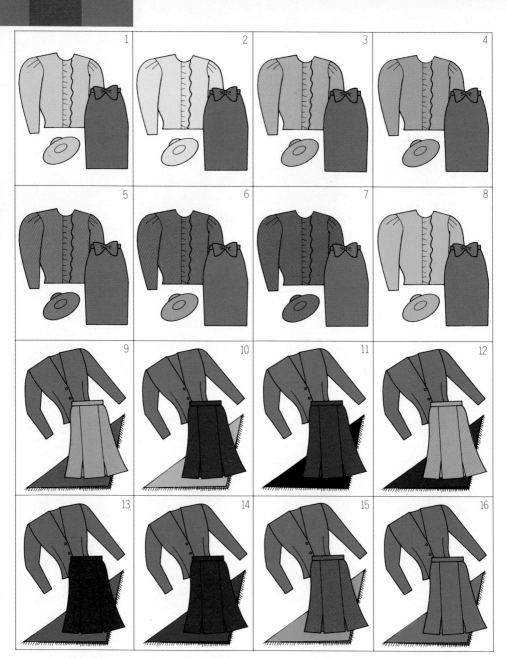

Vary The Tones For Use With Reddish Gray

All of the groupings shown in illustrations 1-16 use a reddish-gray tone as their main color. As shown in the groupings pictured in 5-8, the red tone in the gray helps it blend with bright colors used as secondaries or for accessories. Their brightness adds interest to the gray. The combination shown in illustration 9 is too simple, so try adding a black belt or bag to provide a counterpoint. A printed scarf would help the outfit look brighter. The color grouping shown in 12 is a quiet combination of similar colors with a scarf of an opposing color.

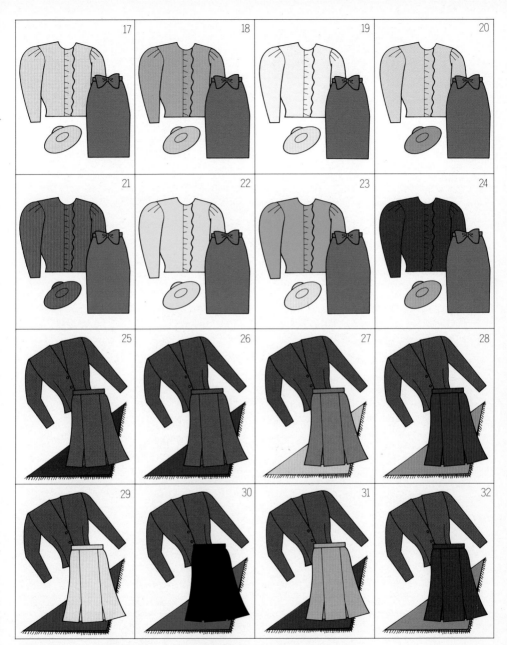

Blue Gray Blends Well With Cool Colors

The color groupings shown in illustrations 17-24 are built around a bluish gray. Like gray, it works with a variety of colors, especially cool ones. The light tones shown in the color schemes illustrated in 17-24 make elegant combinations with blue gray. The groupings shown in 21-24 use vivid colors, presenting an obvious contrast with the low tones of the gray. The purplish gray used in the groupings shown in illustrations 25- 32 is more fashionable than blue gray, but it is harder to coordinate. Use it with black or dark purple to make an easier match.

Monotone & Color

When you classify monochromatics you can say the lightest is white and the darkest is black, while the middle one is medium gray. Between medium gray and black is dark gray. White has traditionally represented fairness, purity, cleanliness and innocence. Black, as the opposite of white, has traditionally been the color of villainy, but today black is treated as favorably as white. As a recent fashion, monochromatics have had a boom, beginning with charcoal gray about 20 years ago. Maybe this is because the clear and simple characteristics of monotones fit with the many artificial elements of the modern environment.

To vary the expression of the color, you can change the texture of the fabric. For example, white silk looks exceedingly white. To make a strong black look hard, make the item in leather.

Monotones harmonize well with other colors, and the monotones can temper them. Used with a strong combination of blue and orange, white softens both colors without ruining either; black makes the combination very sporty; while gray will mediate between the colors and make the outfit quieter.

Monotones match well with almost any color. Black and white can tie together otherwise inharmonious groupings.

1
The stark contrast of black and white looks sharp and modern. Here, a little scarlet is used to spice up the ensemble.

2
Deep blue-purple harmonizes well with monochromatics. This look is urbane and modern.

3
Gray and pink look soft and feminine, but not too sweet. A dark gray accent can be added without "hardening" the effect.

4
This combination uses similar tones. The cool greenish-yellow fits well with gray and white.

5
Here, a vivid green is paired with medium gray, which has the same tonal value. Black is added to enhance the contrast.

6
Black and deep brown are a classic combination. The coolness of black is enhanced by the richness of the brown.

7
Although it is very gray, antique rose will appear more red when worn with a true monochromatic gray.

8
White and gray can be very fresh-looking when worn together. Vivid blue provides a colorful point of emphasis.

Monotone & Pattern

1 A smaller amount of black is used in this large-pattern shepherd's check to keep the overall tone light.

2 Glen plaid, which has a much smaller pattern, gives the impression of medium gray.

A small check pattern made with equal amounts of black and white will appear medium gray, but gives a wholly different impression. If the pattern itself is larger, the impression of black and white is magnified.

7 A white jacket is used with a shepherd check to lighten the tone of the outfit. Use enough white to make an impression.

8 Glen plaid, again, this time combined with a black shirt. The classic design of the outfit emphasizes the black.

3
A black suit with white pinstripes gives the impression of pure black. It matches any monotone except medium gray.

4
This fine check gives the same tonal impression as does the plaid in number 2. A medium gray shirt looks elegant.

5
Here, two patterns are combined in one ensemble. A darker gray blouse is used to highlight the patterns.

6
The black blazer gives this combination of stripes and checks a hard-edged, modern look.

9
A window pane check in black and white makes a sporty impression when worn with a black shirt.

10
This combination is similar to number 4. The pattern makes a strong impression, but use an ample volume of gray.

11
Two different patterns are combined and used as a suit. The design of the pieces is important, and wear a gray shirt.

12
A window pane check and fine check are paired; use them with light gray accessories.

Monotone Pattern & Color

1 Small black polka dots on a white dress make a soft, rhythmic visual impression. The pink jacket brightens the look.

2 A large, bold pattern of black and white creates a dramatic backdrop for this yellow-green shirt.

7 This basic combination of black and white uses neutral beige as a middle ground between the two monochromatic hues.

8 A hint of purple in the gray adds a fashionable twist to this understated combination.

Checks and stripes are coordinated with vivid yellow. The strong image of yellow in the jacket balances the strong patterns. The flared skirt adds an insouciant note to the ensemble.

3

Here, a bold shepherd check is enhanced by a red shirt. Use the same red or black for a hat to complete the ensemble.

4

Blue accessories give this glen plaid outfit an appearance of sportiness and of calm understatement.

5

Rich brown warms up the appearance of this black suit. The two colors complement each other well.

6

Dull olive green adds a masculine twist to this pants suit made of large window-pane check.

9

The different patterns in this combination are tied together by the use of medium gray in both.

10

A very mild, yet interesting and fashionable coordination. Deep red adds drama to the gray of this check pattern.

11

A cool, deep color gives an urbane and elegant air to this combination of large and small checks.

12

Wearing pinstripes with a bright, highly-saturated color can be both sporty and feminine.

Colors Used In This Book

All of the 107 colors used in this book are shown on these two pages. Different colors are shown horizontally while their tones are shown vertically. We have chosen 102 colors and 5 monochromatic hues as a basic

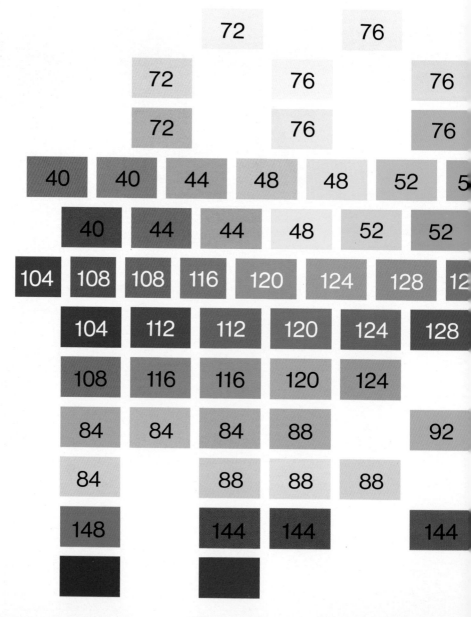

fashion color library.

The first step in improving your sense of color is to master the relationship between these different colors and the subtle distinctions within color families.

The 102 colors are divided into 28 groups.

Typical colors from each group have been chosen as theme colors.

To use the swatch section, first find the color you want to use as a main or theme color on this chart, then turn to the page listed to find colors you can combine it with along with suggestions for types of silhouettes, materials and accents.

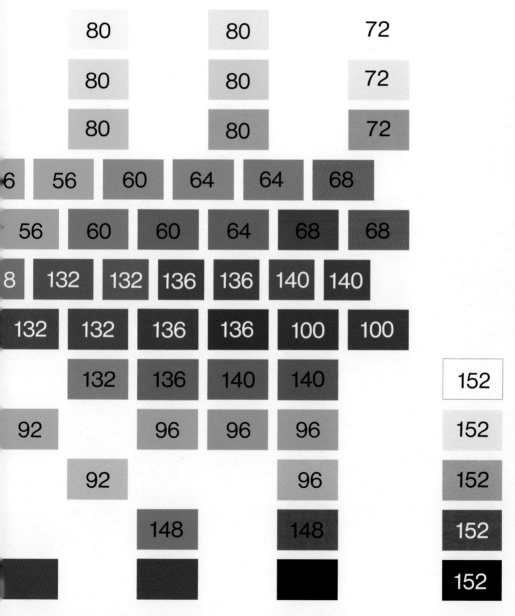

ABOUT THE AUTHORS

Yoko Ogawa

Yoko Ogawa graduated from Joshi Bijutsu Diagaku Art Junior College for Women in 1955 and from Kuwasawa Design School in 1956. She has worked at Kuwasawa Design Kobo Studio in Kobo and at Kurray Co. Ltd. Ms. Ogawa works as a professor at the Kuwasawa Design School and as a lecturer at the Ochanomizu Design School.

Junko Yamamoto

Junko Yamamoto was graduated from Kuwasawa Design School in 1971. Today, she works as an assistant professor at Kuwasawa Design School and as a lecturer for the Women's Fashion Program of Tokyo Fukushoku Bunka Gakoin. She has written *Shin Koko Hifuku* (*New High School Clothing*), *Koko Hifuku Shidosho* (*Guidance for High School Clothing*), published by Jikkyo Shuppan and more.

Ei Kondo

Since graduating from Kuwasawa Design School in 1958, Ei Kondo has worked at Kuwasawa Design School, Tokyo Zokei College. She retired as a professor in 1988 and became a lecturer for the college. Ms. Kondo is a member of The Japan Society for the Science of Design, The International Association of Costume and others.

Editorial Design	Yellow Bag
Illustration	Reiko Saito Naoki Watanabe Koresu Takamura
Editorial Coordinator	Kaoru Takano
Photography	Hideo Imamura
Fashion Coordinate	Ochiai Office
Hair & Make Up	Kimiko Yoshida
Contributors	Ei Robe Takezo Tokyo Blouse Bennetton Mujirushi Ryounin